PEOPLE
OR
PERSONNEL

BOOKS BY PAUL GOODMAN

PEOPLE

OR

PERSONNEL

Decentralizing
and the Mixed System

Paul Goodman

Random House   New York

TO DAVE DELLINGER

Contents

PEOPLE
OR
PERSONNEL

CHAPTER I

Prima Facie Objections

1

Throughout society, the centralizing style of organization has been pushed so far as to become ineffectual, economically wasteful, humanly stultifying, and ruinous to democracy. There are overcentralized systems in industry, in government, in culture, and in agriculture. The tight interlocking of these systems has created a situation in which modest, direct, and independent action has become extremely difficult in every field. The only remedy is a strong admixture of decentralism. The problem is where, how much, and how to go about it.

Let me give some rough definitions. In a centralized enterprise, the function to be performed is the goal of the organization rather than of persons (except as they identify with the organization). The persons are personnel. Authority is top-down. Information is gathered from below in the field and is processed to be usable by those above; decisions are made in headquarters; and policy, schedule, and standard procedure are transmitted downward by chain of command. The enterprise as a whole is divided into departments of operation to which are assigned personnel with distinct roles, to give standard performance. This is the system in Mr. Goldwater's department store, in the Federal government and in the State governments, in General Motors and in the UAW, in the New York public schools and in many universities, in most hospitals, in neighborhood renewal, in network broadcasting and the Associated Press, and in the deals that chain-grocers make with farmers. The system was devised to discipline armies; to keep records, collect taxes, and perform bureaucratic functions; and for certain kinds of mass production. It has now become pervasive.

The principle of decentralism is that people are engaged in a function and the organization is how they cooperate. Authority is delegated away from the top as much as possible and there are many accommodating centers of policy-making and decision. Information is conveyed and discussed in face-to-face contacts between field and headquarters. Each person becomes increasingly aware of the whole operation and works at it in his own way according to his capacities. Groups arrange their own schedules. Historically, this system of voluntary association has yielded most of the values of civilization, but it is thought to be entirely unworkable under modern conditions and the very sound of it is strange.

2

Now if, lecturing at a college, I happen to mention that some function of society which is highly centralized could be much decentralized without loss of efficiency, or perhaps with a gain in efficiency, at once the students want to talk about nothing else. This insistence of theirs used to surprise me, and I tested it experimentally by slipping in a decentralist remark during lectures on entirely different subjects. The students unerringly latched on to the remark. In their questions, for twenty minutes they might pursue the main theme —*e.g.* nuclear pacifism or even the sexual revolution— but they returned to decentralization for many hours, attacking me with skepticism, hot objections, or hard puzzlers.

From their tone, it is clear that in this subject something is at stake for their existence. They feel trapped in the present system of society that allows them so little say or initiative, and that indeed is like the schooling that they have been enduring for twelve to sixteen years. The querulousness and biting sarcasm mean that, if decentralization *is* possible, they have become needlessly resigned; they hotly defend the second best that they have opted for instead. But the serious and hard questions are asked with a tone of skeptical wistfulness that *I* will be able to resolve all difficulties. If I confess at some point that I don't know the answer, at once students invent answers for me, to prove that decentralization *is* possible after all.

Naturally, at each college we go over much the same ground. The very sameness of the discussions is disheartening evidence that the centralist style exists as a mass-superstition, never before questioned in the students' minds. If I point to some commonplace defect of any centralized system, or one which leaps to the eye in the organization of their own college, I am regarded as a daring sage. No other method of organization was conceived as possible.

I shall devote this first chapter to these usual preliminary objections.

3

Decentralization is not lack of order or planning, but a kind of coordination that relies on different motives from top-down direction, standard rules, and extrinsic rewards like salary and status, to provide integration and cohesiveness. It is not "anarchy." (But of course, most Anarchists, like the anarcho-syndicalists or the community-anarchists, have not been "anarchists" either, but decentralists.)

As an example of decentralist coordination, the Anarchist Prince Kropotkin, who was a geographer, used to point spectacularly to the history of Western science from the heroic age of Vesalius, Copernicus, and Galileo to his own time of Pasteur, Kelvin, and J. J. Thomson. The progress of science in all fields was exquisitely coordinated. There were voluntary associations, publications, regional and international conferences. The Ph. D. system was devised to disseminate new research to several hundred university libraries. There was continual private correspondence, even across warring boundaries. Yet in this vast common enterprise, so amazingly productive, there was no central direction whatever.

The chief bond of cohesion was, of course, that all scientists had the common aim of exploring Nature, as well as their personal idiosyncrasies and their personal and clique rivalries. The delicate integration of effort occurred because they followed the new data or worked with the frontier theories. It was almost uniquely rare, so far as we know (the case of Mendel is famous), that important work dropped out of the dialogue.

In the past forty years, the organization of science has begun to rely heavily on central Institutes and Foundations, to choose areas of research, to select personnel, to grant funds. National governments have become the chief sponsors and, in a sense, directors of research. It is possible that, on balance, this mode of organization might produce better results. It is efficient in that there are, literally, more "scientists" and there is a proliferation of research products. Without doubt some methods, like population surveys, and some apparatus, like atom smashers and moon rockets, require a lot of capital and central organization. It has been argued that when knowledge accumulates beyond a certain point, its dissemination must be centrally directed and further research must be systematically directed.

Yet it is not self-evident that this style is superior to the private industriousness, lonely thought, shoe-string apparatus of Pasteur, Edison, and Einstein, or the master-disciple relations of Thomson, Rutherford, etc. Proof is difficult either way, for if the best brains are working in one style we cannot tell what they would be doing if working in another style. Even in technology and in the modern, centralized climate, as Ben Seligman has pointed out, "Since 1900, about half of the important inventions affecting consumer goods have come from independent researchers. Air-conditioning, automatic transmissions, cellophane, jet engines, and quick-freeze came from old-fashioned inventors or small companies."

The ideal test would be to try out both styles, but in fact the big central style eventually drives out the other, by non-scientific pressures. It buys up persons, dictates to the universities by grants for research and development, piles administrative and consultant duties on keen minds that would otherwise be working in philosophical seclusion or in real teaching. Some of the disadvantages are obvious. With the best will in the world, when so much capital and organization are invested there is a tendency toward immediate profits and military power, and there appears—astoundingly, in the history of Western science—commercial and political secrecy as a condition of research. Under authoritative direction, and with extrinsic rewards, a vast amount of "research" has been mere busywork. The pursuit of the goals of the organization, in "crash" programs, whether in medicine, strategy, or space exploration, necessarily has a different principle of order than the wandering dialogue of intellect with the unknown nature of things.

4

Over the centuries, not only scientific truth but most other objective values, like beauty or compassion, have thrived by voluntary association and independent solitude. (Theological salvation is perhaps the only spiritual good that has usually been centrally regulated.) Almost by definition, the progress of social justice has been by voluntary association, since the central authority is what is rebelled against. And, of course, to preserve liberty, the American political system was deliberately designed as a polarity of centralist and decentralist elements, with limitations on the power of the Sovereign and in-built checks and balances at every level.

But we must also remember that in its heyday, celebrated by Adam Smith, the free-enterprise system of partnerships and vigilant joint stockholders was in theory a model of decentralist coordination, as opposed to the centralized system of mercantilism, royal patents, and monopolies that it replaced. It reposed an absolute reliance on self-interest, voluntary association, and the cohesive influence of natural forces: Economic Man and the Laws of the Market. Pretty soon, however, the stockholders stopped attending to business and became absentee investors or even gamblers on the stock exchange. And almost from the beginning in this country, notably in the bank and the tariff, there was a revival of state monopolies.

5

"How can you decentralize air-traffic control?" asks a student.

You can't. There are many functions that are central by their natures, and it is useful to enumerate some of the chief kinds.

Central authority is necessary where there are no district limits and something positive must be done, as in epidemic control or smog control; or when an arbitrary decision is required and there is no time for reflection, as in traffic control; or when we have to set arbitrary standards for a whole field, but the particular standard is indifferent, *e.g.* weights and measures or money.

Centralization is temporarily necessary when an emergency requires the concentration of all powers in a concerted effort. But history has shown that such emergency centralization can be fateful, for the central organization tends to outlive the emergency, and then its very existence creates a chronic emergency; people soon become helpless unless they are told what to do.

Central authority is convenient to perform routine or "merely" administrative functions, when people have more important things to do. This is the Marxist theory of the withering away of the State to "mere" administration. But this too can be fateful, for administration soon encroaches on every function. It is thus that the executive secretary of an organization ends up running the show.

Central organization is the most rational kind when

the logistics of a situation outweigh consideration of the concrete particulars involved. These are all the cases of ticketing and tax collecting, where one person is like another. (*E.g.* a train ticket is technically a contract, but it would be absurd to negotiate each ticket individually.) In my opinion, the same holds for the mass production and distribution of any standard item that is good enough and that everybody needs.

Besides, there are monopolies that must be regulated and licensed by central authority (or nationalized), since by definition they cannot be countervailed. Some monopolies are natural or become so by circumstances, like urban water supply. Some enterprises become monopolistic because they are so heavily capitalized that competition is prohibitively risky or wasteful. They grow until they become the inevitable nature of things, and then must be so regulated. For instance, the railroads of Europe were decentrally planned and constructed, with voluntary agreement on gauges and schedules; but eventually, as monopolies, they have been nationalized and partly internationalized.

My bias is decentralist, yet in some functions I think we need more centralization than we have. For instance, there ought to be uniform modular standards in building materials and fixtures. Building is a typical example of how we do things backwards. Where there ought to be decentralization, for instance in the design which requires artistry and in the decision of each neighborhood on how it wants to live, we get bureaucratic routine design, national policy, the standards of absentee sociologists, and the profits of promoters. But where there could be important savings, in materials and the process of construction, we do not standardize. Similarly, there ought to be standard-

ization of machine parts and design, especially for
domestic machinery and cars, to make repairs easier.
And it is certainly absurd for the expensive enterprise
of space exploration to be internationally competitive,
instead of centrally planned and departmentalized
with crews and honors shared.

Finally, automatic and computer technology is by
nature highly centralizing, in its style and in its applications. This is a massive phenomenon of the present and
immediate future and we shall recur to it continually
(especially in Chapter VI). In general, the point of
view of this book is that, where it is relevant, this
technology should be maximized as quickly as possible and many such plants should be regulated as
monopolies. But perhaps the profoundest problem
that faces modern society is to decide *in what functions the automatic and computer style is not relevant,
and there to curtail it or forget it.*

Thus, it is reasonable to use business machines in a
branch-library system to expedite finding and exchang-
ing books among the branches. But in my opinion, it is
more dubious to select the books centrally and by computer, according to standards of excellence, consensus
of the national reviews, etc.; for selection is a chief
means of education and avenue of self-expression for
each branch-librarian, and local attention is indispensable for the specific cultivation of each neighborhood.
And in the children's section, even routine checking in
and out provides unembarrassed occasions for conversation between the librarian and the children.

6

A Marxist student objects that blurring the division
of labor, local option, face-to-face communication,
and other decentralist positions are relics of a peasant
ideology, provincial and illiberal.

There is something in this. In fact, there have always been two strands to decentralist thinking. Some authors, *e.g.* Lao-tse or Tolstoy, make a conservative peasant critique of centralized court and town as inorganic, verbal, and ritualistic. But other authors, *e.g.* Proudhon or Kropotkin, make a democratic urban critique of centralized bureaucracy and power, including feudal industrial power, as exploiting, inefficient, and discouraging to initiative. In our present era of State socialism, corporate feudalism, regimented schooling, brainwashing mass communications, and urban anomie, both kinds of critique make sense. We need to revive both peasant self-reliance and the democratic power of professional and technical guilds and workers' councils.

Any decentralization that could occur at present would inevitably be post-urban and post-centralist; it could not be provincial. There is no American who has not been formed by national TV, and no region that has not been homogenized by the roads and chain stores. A model of twentieth-century decentralization is the Israeli *kibbutz*. Some would say that these voluntary communities are fanatical, but no one would deny that they are cosmopolitan and rationalistic, post-centralist and post-urban.

Decentralizing has its risks. Suppose that the school system of a Northern city were radically decentralized, given over to the control of the parents and teachers of each school. Without doubt some of the schools would be Birchite and some would be badly neglected. Yet it is hard to imagine that many schools could be worse than the present least-common-denominator. There would certainly be more experimentation. There would be meaningful other choices to move to. And inevitably all the schools would exist in a framework of general standards that they would have to measure up to or suffer the consequences.

Invariably, some student argues that without the intervention of the Federal government, the Negroes in the South will not get their civil rights. This may or may not be so, but certainly most of their progress toward civil rights so far has come from local action that has embarrassed and put pressure on Washington. By the same token the Negro organizations themselves have been decentrally coordinated; as Dr. King has pointed out, the "leadership" is continually following the localities. But the basic error of this student is to think that the "States' Rights" of the segregationists is decentralist. (An authentic regionalism *would* be decentralist.) If each locality indeed had its option, the counties where Negroes are in the majority would have very different rules! And they would provide a meaningful choice for other Negroes to move to.

7

The relation of decentralization to physical and social mobility is an important topic; let us stay with it for another page. As the example of science has shown, it is possible to have decentralist community without territorial community. Yet decentralist philosophies have prized stability, "rootedness," subtle awareness of the environment, as a means to the integration of the domestic, technical, economic, political, and cultural functions of life, and to provide a physical community in which the young can grow up.

The Americans have always been quick to form voluntary associations—Tocqueville mentions the trait with admiration; yet Americans have always been mobile—usually going *away*, individuals and families leaving communities that did not offer opportunity, in order to try new territory known by hearsay. Historically, the country was open at the margins, because of either the geographical frontier or new jobs that attracted immigrants. When people settled, they again formed voluntary associations. Thus, to a degree, voluntary mobility favored decentralization. On the other hand, the new ties and settlements inevitably tended to become more homogeneous and national, the result of any uprooting.

At present, however, the country is closed at the margins, yet the physical (and social) mobility is even greater. Negroes migrate north because the sharecropping has failed and they are barred from the factories; Northern middle-class whites move to the suburbs to escape the Negroes; farm families have dwindled to 8 per cent. Unfortunately, none of these groups is moving *to* anything. And much moving is ordered by the central organization itself: national corporations send their employees and families to this or that branch; universities raid one another for staff; promoters and bureaucrats dislocate tenants for urban redevelopment.

Under such conditions people must end up in total anomie, with no meaningful relation to the environment and society. There seem to be two alternative remedies. One was proposed forty years ago by Le Corbusier: to centralize and homogenize completely, so that one dwelling place is exactly like another, with identical furniture, services, and surroundings. When all live in identical hotel rooms, mobility does not involve much dislocation. The other alternative is to build communities where meaningful voluntary association is again possible; that is, to decentralize. This has, of course, been the wistful aim of suburbanism,

and it continually appears in the real-estate advertise-
ments. But a suburb is not a decentralist community;
its purposes, way of life, and decisions are determined
by business headquarters, the national standard of living, and the bureau of highways. The hope of community is in people deciding important matters for
themselves.

8

A student raises a related objection: Decentralism is
for small towns; it cannot work with big dense populations. But I don't think this objection has any merit.
Decentralism is a kind of social organization; it does
not involve geographical isolation, but a particular sociological use of geography.

In important respects, a city of five million can be
decentrally organized as many scores of unique communities in the framework of a busy metropolis.

Usually in modern urban administration, the various
municipal functions—school, job induction, social
work, health, police and court for misdemeanors, post
office, housing and rent control, election district, etc.
—are divided into units only for the administrative
convenience of City Hall. The districts do not coin-
cide with one another or with neighborhoods. A citizen with business or complaint must seek out the district office of each department, or perhaps go to City
Hall. And correspondingly, there is no possible forum
to discuss the coordination of the various functions
except at the very top, with the Mayor or before the
City Council.

Decentralist organization would rather follow the
actuality of living in an urban community, where housing, schooling, shopping, policing, social services, politics are integrally related. Each neighborhood should
have a local City Hall. Such *arrondissements* could

have considerable autonomy within the municipal administration that controls transit, sanitation, museums, etc., whatever is necessarily or conveniently centralized. Taxes could be collected centrally and much of the take divided among the neighborhoods to be budgeted locally.

For the average citizen, the convergence of all kinds of related business in one local center is not only convenient but must lead to more acquaintance and involvement. Poor people especially do not know their way around, are stymied by forms to fill out, and have no professional help; they are defeated by fighting City Hall and soon give up. Besides, each neighborhood has interlocking problems peculiar to itself. These can be reasonably confronted by citizens and local officials, but they are lost in the inner politics of central bureaucracies that have quite different axes to grind.

For instance, a neighborhood so constituted might learn to decide on its own redevelopment. In programs for urban renewal, the Federal government follows the traditional formula of balancing centralism and decentralism and asks for approval of plans by the local community. Cities therefore set up local "planning boards." But this works out as follows. Occasionally, middle-class residential neighborhoods can organize themselves to prevent any change whatever; poor people are entirely passive to the powers-that-be; most usually, the boards are rubber stamps for City Hall and promoters. The say of a neighborhood in its destiny can be meaningful only if the neighborhood has begun to be conscious of itself as a community. For this, mere "consent" or "participation" is not enough; there must be a measure of real initiating and deciding, grounded in acquaintance and trust.

However, the question is not whether decentralization can work in dense urban populations, but how to make it work, for it is imperative. The increase of urban social disease and urban mental disease is fundamentally due to powerlessness, resignation, and withdrawal, as if people's only way to assert vitality is to develop symptoms. The central authorities try to cope as stern or hygienic caretakers; the citizens respond by becoming "community-dependent"—in jail, in the hospital, on relief; that is, they become chronic patients. With many, this has gone on for two and three generations.

9

Yet something further needs to be said about big dense populations. In my opinion, there is a limit of urban density and urban sprawl beyond which *no* form of social organization, centralist or decentralist, can cope. Urban crowding creates a peculiar climate of both too many social relations and a kind of sensory and emotional deprivation. Instead of contact and communication, there is noise and withdrawal. It is no different from John Calhoun's overcrowded rodents who become confused and die. It is as if the circuits are clogged. Similarly, Harrison Matthews has shown that many mammals who in the wild are peaceful, become hostile in the "urban conditions" of a zoo, where there is not enough "social space" to experiment with their territoriality and hierarchy. Another naturalist, Loren Eiseley, says, "The higher the human population mounts, the more humanity in its behavior resembles the jostlings of the molecules of a gas under confined circumstances. It is not out of such confinement that a truly human future can be assured." For instance, the density of population in Central Harlem, at 67,000 per square mile, is nearly three times that of New York City as a whole. Even apart from the other unfavorable conditions of the Negroes, such crowding itself is pathological, overstimulating yet culturally impoverishing, destructive of solitude, excessively and brutally policed.

Our degree of urbanization is beyond reason. In this country we have the symptoms of a "population explosion" at the same time that vast and beautiful rural regions have become depopulated. We shall see (Chapter III) how, in the present setup, only big operators with migrant labor can make a go of farming, and how the farm subsidies work disproportionately in favor of this group. Except for a few earnest but powerless voices, there is a general agreement to let farming-as-a-way-of-life die out. Yet no effort whatever is made to find urban substitutes for the independence, multifarious skill, community spirit, and extended family that were rural values.

During the Great Depression, the Roosevelt Administration made some efforts to support subsistence farming, as a factor of social stability and to relieve both rural and urban misery. But with the return of Prosperity, nothing further came of it. (We shall refer again to the shaggy decentralism of parts of the early New Deal. In Appendix III, I make a New Deal-like proposal.)

10

A student hotly objects that decentralism is humanly unrealistic, it "puts too much faith in human nature" by relying on intrinsic motives, like interest in the job and voluntary association. Another student mentions Rousseau, who is still academically out of fashion since his debunking by Professor Babbitt a generation ago. (Jefferson, too, is now getting his lumps.)

This objection is remarkably off-base. My experience is that most decentralists are crotchety and skeptical and tend rather to follow Aristotle than Rousseau. We must avoid concentration of power precisely because we *are* fallible; *quis custodiet custodes?* Democracy, Aristotle says, is to be preferred because it is the "least evil" form of government, since it divides power among many. I think the student states the moral issue upside down. The moral question is not whether men are "good enough" for a type of social organization, but whether the type of organization is useful to develop the potentialities of intelligence, grace, and freedom in men.

More deeply, the distrust of "human nature," of course, is anxious conformism. One must save face, not make a mistake in any detail; so one clings to an assigned role. But, unfortunately, the bigger the organization, the more face to save. For instance, we shall see that the government Peace Corps is many times as expensive as similar less official operations largely because an errant twenty-year-old well-digger might become an International Incident, so one cannot be too careful in selecting him. Convenience of supervision overrides performance. And the more "objective" the better. If the punch card approves, no one is guilty. To bureaucrats, a fatal hallmark of decentralist enterprises is their variety in procedure and persons; how can one *know*, with a percentage validity, that these methods and persons are *right?*

Morally, all styles of social organization are self-proving, for people understand the rightness of what everybody in fact does. But different styles have different norms. The centralizing style makes for both petty conforming and admiration for bigness. The more routine and powerless people are, the more they are mesmerized by extrinsic proofs of production and power. An enterprise that is designed on a small scale for a particular need of particular people comes to be regarded as though it were nothing at all. To win attention and support, it must call itself a Pilot Project, promising mighty applications.

Nevertheless, still deeper than these neurotic confusions, there is, in my opinion, an authentic confusion in the face of unprecedented conditions of modern times, that makes for rigidity and fear of social experiment. A student says, "We could afford to experiment if it were not for the Chinese, the Cubans, the crime rate, the unemployment, the space race, the population explosion." The leap in technology, the galloping urbanization, nuclear weapons, the breakdown of the colonial system—all involve threats and dilemmas. The inevitable response of people is to rally to the style of strict control by experts. In emergencies, centralized organization seems to make sense and often does make sense. It is also comfortingly dictatorial.

11

Finally, the moral objection is stated also the opposite way: decentralizing is impossible, not because people are incapable but because the powers-that-be won't allow it. (This student is an Angry Young Man.) Granting that in some areas decentralization is workable, how could it possibly be brought about? We cannot expect central powers to delegate autonomy any more than we can expect the nation-states to give up any of their sovereignty and grandeur. Indeed, the tendency is entirely in the other direction, toward bigger corporations, combinations, and tie-ins, toward tighter scheduling and grading in education, toward increased standardization and the application of automatic and computer technology in every field, and of course toward the increase of power in Washington to become the greatest landlord, the greatest sponsor of research, and the greatest policeman.

Yes. But there are forces also in the opposite direction. I must assume, for instance, that it is not a social accident that I, as an author, am writing this book.

In principle, there are two ways in which an over-centralized system can become more mixed. Voluntary associations form spontaneously because of pressing needs to which the central system is irrelevant or antipathetic. Or the central authority itself chooses, or is forced, to build in decentral parts because its method is simply not working.

There is a marked trend toward spontaneous associations that indicates first a despair of, and then an indifference to, the regular methods. One must "do it oneself." We have already noticed the spontaneity, localism, and decentralist federation of the Negro civil rights movement, as different from the more conventional maneuvering of the Urban League and the older NAACP. But this is part of a general spread of para-legal demonstrating, boycotting, and show of power that express dissent with formal procedures that are not effective. The great discovery has been non-violent activism, and this is peculiarly epidemic, for it immediately provides something to do rather than merely being balked—a beautiful feature of it, often, is to balk the authorities who have been balking us; yet it does not require forming political parties or organizing private armies. (When non-violence is morally authentic, indeed, its very action is decentralizing: it restores the opposition to being persons rather than personnel. Violence has the contrary effect, of welding people into rigid organizations.)

Do-It-Yourself can be para-institutional if not overtly para-legal. Beat youth withdraws from the economy and tries to contrive a community culture of its own. Off-Broadway first withdraws from Broadway, dissident artists first withdraw from the big commercial galleries and set up their own galleries, etc.; but then there spreads a distaste for formal showings altogether. Students quit famous universities because they decide they are not being educated; then they form, for instance, the Northern Student Movement in order to tutor backward urban children; but then the Northern Student Movement decides that the public school curriculum is inadequate, and the tutors will teach according to their own lights. Freedom Now sets up what amounts to a para-party in Mississippi.

And there is a similar tone even within the political framework. Contrasted with older "reform" movements which were devoted to purging the bosses and grafters, the new urban reform movements rapidly constitute themselves *ad hoc* for a concrete purpose other than getting hold of the party machinery, usually to block outrageous encroachments of government or big institutions. (Unfortunately, however, these reform "movements" usually do not have a counter-program; they stop with exercising a veto, lose steam, and eventually lose the original issue too. We shall mention an exception in Chapter IV.)

All this kind of ferment is what Arthur Waskow, of the Institute for Policy Studies, calls "creative disorder."

But also, as I shall spell out in the next chapter, the startling strength of know-nothing movements in the country is importantly due to justified dissatisfaction with the centralization, exactly as they claim when they reiterate the slogan, "Government must not do what people can do for themselves." By "people" our reactionary friends seem mainly to mean corporations, which are not people, yet I do not think that liberals and progressives pay attention to the underlying gripe, the loss of self-determination. The liberals glibly repeat that the complex problems of modern times do not allow simplistic solutions; no, they don't; but what is the use of "rational" solutions which finally are not the solutions of one's underlying problem?

12

I do not notice any significant disposition of central powers to decentralize themselves. Rather, when the organization begins to creak, their disposition is to enlarge it further by adding new bureaus and overseers, to stall by appointing committees without power, to disregard difficulties and hope they will go away, or to call hard cases "deviant" and put them out of circulation.

Nevertheless, there are examples to show how decentralization *can* be built in.

The management of a giant corporation—General Motors is the classic example—can shrewdly decide to delegate a measure of autonomy to its corporate parts, because more flexible enterprising is more profitable in the long run. Similarly, a huge physical plant can be geographically dispersed, and the management somewhat decentralized, to save on labor costs and get better tax breaks. In the Soviet Union, correspondingly, there is pressure for regional industrial councils, especially for allocating consumer goods. Naturally, these motives do nothing at all for the great majority of subordinates, though they multiply vice-presidents and local commissars.

More interesting for our purposes is the multifarious application of industrial psychology. For the most part, the psychologists are decentralist by disposition and have taught a wisdom opposite to the time-motion studies of "scientific business management." Rather than subdividing the workman further and departmentalizing further, they have urged that it is efficient to allow more choice and leeway, to ask for suggestions from below, to increase "belonging." To give a typical example: In one plant it has been found more productive in the long run for half a dozen workmen to assemble a big lathe from beginning to end and have the satisfaction of seeing it carried away, than to subdivide the operation on a line.

Needless to say, our industrial psychologists cannot pursue their instincts to the logical conclusion, workers' management. Yet questions of degree are *not* trivial. Consider the following example: In an area of England, it is traditional to work by a gang or collective contract. (This "Coventry system" has been studied by Professor Melman of Columbia.) A group of workmen agree to complete in a period a certain quantity of piecework, for which they are paid a sum of money divided equally. The capitalist provides the machinery and materials, but everything else—work rules, schedule, hiring—is left to group decision. The group may be half a dozen or a couple of thousand. Humanly, such an arrangement has extraordinary advantages. Men exchange jobs and acquire new skills; they adjust the schedule to their convenience or pleasures; they bring in and train apprentices; they invent labor-saving devices, which are to their own advantage; they cover for one another when sick or for special vacations.

Obviously such a system, so amazingly at variance with our minute top-down regulation, time-clock discipline, labor-union details, and competitive spirit, is hard to build into most of American industry. Yet where it would suit, it would make a profound difference. Where would it suit? How could it be tailored? How to get it put into effect?

Sometimes Federal or State agencies have to rely on

decentralist organizations to make their own operations feasible. "Community developers" are sent in, *e.g.* by Mobilization for Youth; or just come in, like Saul Alinsky. State-aided housing involves developing Tenants' Councils to give the families a means of complaint against the sponsors and of petition to the State.

In the recent student disorders at Berkeley, there was a remarkable resurgence of initiative by the Faculty, just to make communication again possible, for the Administration was obviously entirely out of touch. The Faculty then sought to resume faculty control of student discipline, but as of this writing (December 1964) the Regents have refused this.

The occasional attempts at University reform, to alleviate the regimenting by the credits and grading machine, have been decentral structures like in-built honors colleges or the federation of small colleges instead of unlimited expansion. (But we have not yet come to the wisdom of breaking up the sixteen-year interlocked school system and offering alternative ways of growing up and different speeds for education.)

An attempt to build in decentralization has recently been occurring in the New York public school system. Because of a combination of near-riots in poor neighborhoods, some spectacular run-of-the-mill scandals, and the post-sputnik spotlight on upgrading, a new and pretty good Board was appointed. Deciding that the system is overcentralized, these gentlemen have resuscitated twenty-five local districts—averaging more than forty thousand children each!—and appointed local boards with rather indefinite powers, to serve as liaison to the neighborhoods. But unlike the case of the Urban Renewal Planning Boards mentioned above, the intention has been to delegate positive powers; and, anyway, the remarkably strong-minded body of people who have been appointed to the local school boards have declined to be rubber stamps. For a couple of years now, there has been a jockeying for position and power. The local boards are empowered to hold budget hearings and "suggest" allocation of money. What does this mean? Could they "suggest" to eliminate some of the curriculum and services and substitute others? Some local board members want to decentralize radically, making the field superintendents (with their advisory boards) nearly autonomous within the big system, as is reasonable, since different neighborhoods have different conditions and must therefore have different curricula, staff, and service needs.

One of the Manhattan boards, curious to know what its sister boards were doing, convened a meeting of the five Manhattan boards, and they agreed to exchange minutes. At once central headquarters protested and forbade such attempts at federation. "If you issue joint statements," headquarters pointed out, "people will think that you speak for the school system." "What can you do about it?" asked the locals; "since you have called us into existence, we exist, and since we exist, we intend to act." I mention this incident not because it is important in itself, but because it is at the heart of the constitutional problem of centralization and decentralization.

13

These, then, are the chief *prima facie* objections raised by college students. Decentralization is disorderly and "anarchic." You cannot decentralize air-traffic control and public health. What about automation? Decentralization is a peasant ideology. It makes for "States' Rights" injustice. It is unworkable with big dense populations. It implies an unrealistic faith that human nature is good and human beings are reasonable. It is impossible to go against the overwhelming trend toward bigness and power.

What is most discouraging in such discussions is that students keep referring to "your system" or "the decentralist system."

But I am not proposing a system. It is hard to convince college students that it is improbable that there *could* be a single appropriate style of organization or economy to fit all the functions of society, any more than there could—or ought to be—a single mode of education, "going to school," that suits almost everybody; or any more than there is a "normal" psychology that is healthy for almost everybody.

Rather, it seems to me as follows. We are in a period of excessive centralization. In this book I shall try to demonstrate that in many functions this style is economically inefficient, technologically unnecessary, and humanly damaging. Therefore we might adopt a political *maxim:* to decentralize where, how, and how much is expedient. But where, how, and how much are *empirical* questions. They require research and experiment.

In the existing overcentralized climate of opinion, it is just this research and experiment that we are not getting. Among all the departments, agencies, and commissions in Washington, I have not heard of one that deals with the organizational *style* of municipalities, social work, manufacturing, merchandising, or education in terms of technical and economic efficiency and effect on persons. Therefore, I urge students who are going on to graduate work to choose their theses in this field.

CHAPTER II

The Sentiment of Powerlessness in American History

1

Feeling that the present social style is stifling them, college students are interested in decentralist ideas as an alternative. There is no such interest among the voting citizens. In the political spectrum from Left to Right, all shades share the belief in top-down management. Liberals believe in more rather than less Federal intervention in this management; "conservatives" would rather leave it to the corporations, which are a kind of feudal baronies. (The term "conservative" in our politics tends to mean back to McKinley. Strict constitutionalists like Black are regarded as radical. And those who would conserve the natural environment and human freedom to breathe and initiate are, at present, usually anarchists.)

A generation ago, intellectual liberals used to express enthusiasm for a "mixed economy." The model was Sweden which enjoyed, it was said, a mixture of welfare-state socialism, independent enterprise, corporate enterprise, a strong cooperative movement, and a stable balance of farm and city. In this mixture, the cooperatives, the independents, and the small farms were decentralist components, and they were a power against engulfment by State and corporations.

The mixed system is no longer mentioned. Not since the Populism of 1890 has this country had any spirit for producers' cooperatives. During the past thirty years consumers' cooperatives have lost headway, and even the service of consumer information, *e.g.* the Consumers' Union, has retrogressed and been left to the Federal government. Everybody agrees, and legislates, to drive small farms out of existence. And there are no longer many independents—*e.g.* less than 2 per cent of college graduates go into independent enterprises, but 35 per cent into the corporations and an even greater number into government service and teaching in the public systems or great universities. Even the majority of professionals become "professional personnel."

Liberals do not now think that anybody is engulfed and needs a recourse to exercise initiative. Their strategy for helping the powerless is not to cut things down to size or open spaces to breathe, but to spend money on schools, welfare, retraining, area redevelopment, managed from above. The powerless become clients. Astoundingly, liberals no longer even talk about civil liberties, though there is endless talk about civil rights. That is, one is entitled to due process within the central organization, but one is not protected in going one's own way.

The regulatory agencies, sponsored by the older liberalism, have become accommodations with the giant monopolies, rather than means of pluralizing. And of course liberal government has itself become a giant entrepreneur, in highways, housing, research and devel-

opment, space exploration. Not to mention the sixty-
billion-dollar budget for Defense, which is managed by
whatever government, Democratic or Republican.
(With a modest multiplier, this budget for Defense
controls a quarter of the entire economy.)

Accordingly, there is a major new class of bureaucratized intellectuals, a kind of monkhood. These are
the professors, sociologists, contracted researchers,
diplomates, licensed social workers, consultants, think-
factory hands, and other doctors of philosophy and
professional-personnel who provide the reasoning and
rationalizations for the centralizing programs of liberal
government.

2

Oddly, the rhetoric of independence and civil liberties is now spoken only by Big Business, at least by the
branches of Big Business that are not immediate part-
ners of government and operating on cost-plus. But the
tone of Business rhetoric is no longer the social-
Darwinism of rugged individualism, but rather defen-
sive complaint against the encroachment of the *other*
entrepreneur. The usual substance is the wish for
lower taxes, less regulation, and the elimination of the
corporation of Labor; often, however, one can detect a
direct clash of rival combinations, *e.g.* Steel-Oil-Air-
craft *vs.* Electronics-M. I. T.-National Science Foundation.

This ancient war of the King and the Barons has little to do with decentralization in the meaning of this
book, nor indeed with personal liberty. Let me tell an
anecdote. I was on a panel with the publisher of the
National Review, and he complained grievously about
Mr. Kennedy's police harassment of the head of U. S.
Steel. I was sympathetic, and I told him about a couple
of Puerto Ricans in New York who were treated even

worse, actually manhandled. But I could not get him interested in their case.

I doubt that at present, on balance, the more or less intervention of Federal government is unfavorable or favorable to free enterprise in any important human sense.

In this chapter, I shall be mainly describing the growth of Federal centralization, with the corporations aiding and abetting. In the next chapter, my examples will be drawn from non-Federal centralization, with the Federal government aiding and abetting. The net result is similar.

3

Nevertheless, although it is hypocritical, the conservative rhetoric about encroachment is important, and perhaps dangerous, because it is true. All classes believe in the inevitability of universal top-down direction in one form or another, but people are also restive at their powerlessness. And this restiveness is especially acute in two great strata of the middle class, those who are losing out (including small farmers), and those who are precariously climbing, anxious suburbanites often educated beyond their capacities. These groups are inflamed by the anti-centralist rhetoric which they accept, personally, in its most extreme statements—anti-Negro, anti-urban, anti-sociological, and jingoist. They thus constitute a fascist threat, not in the name of Order but of Liberty! To be sure, they are not consistent. We are told that extremism in the defense of liberty is no vice; but progressive education or giving the accused a fair shake in court is not liberty but License.

By the usual irony of history, the Big Business rhetoric of today is rather like the rhetoric of Populism, including its know-nothing excesses, that was invented just to break out of the centralizing trap of Big Business.

Conversely, the rhetoric of Liberalism has become paternalistic and moderate, and promises to lead us right to 1984.

To find how this extraordinary switch has come about, let us make a quick survey of American history from the beginning. Our theme is the growth among citizens of a feeling of powerlessness to initiate and decide.

4

When the American Revolution removed the British authority at the top, society remained mainly organized as a network of highly structured face-to-face communities and associations, and these were fairly autonomous. The structures were sometimes democratic; more often they were little clusters around an elite. There were town meetings, congregational parishes, yeoman families, masters and apprentices, masters and indentured servants, gentry families with hired help and slaves, professionals and their clients. Democratic or hierarchic, the groups were small, and on most matters people were in frequent personal contact with those who initiated and decided.

It is astoundingly likely, however, that with respect to the State or confederated government, during the first twenty-five or thirty years of the Republic these communities existed in a virtual community-anarchy. The franchise was heavily restricted by requirements of property, education, sex, religion, and color; but the interesting evidence is that very few of those who were enfranchised bothered to vote anyway, often only one or two per cent of the population. Nevertheless, the general sentiment and rhetoric are intensely democratic, sometimes egalitarian.

No such anarchist picture appears in our histories; but, of course, they are written to highlight either the previous war or the breakdown of the Articles of Confederation or the *prospective* importance of the Federal government in the next century, or else particular major Federal actions, like the Northwest Ordinance, the Sedition Laws, or the Louisiana Purchase. It is not much mentioned, *e.g.*, that for a couple of years Jefferson abolished the navy as useless; or that once Shays' Rebellion was dispersed, it was entirely condoned. (Jefferson to Madison: "A little rebellion now and then is a good thing. . . . This truth should render republican governors so mild in their punishment of rebellions as not to discourage them.")

One has the impression that unless a man engaged in interstate or international commerce or was a creditor and had to do with lawyers, he was quite indifferent to what went on in government. Formally, the total sovereignty had devolved on the States; but how much addition of positive powers did this imply? Except for matters of high culture—where it was of major importance—the departure of the British seems to have left few gaps and simply removed unnecessary clogs to life. This is certainly the implication of Richard Henry Lee's complaint that, in 1787, a Constitution was entirely premature; all that was needed was the regulation of trade, of legal tender, and of fraudulent debtors and "men unfriendly to Republican equality."

5

Yet these "anarchist" communities were *not* nonpolitical. Quite the contrary! Especially the independent elite regarded themselves as a band of citizen-friends born to make institutions, constitutions, or whatever. The rhetoric of the Declaration of Independence, and the act itself, were momentous just because they had this existential spontaneity; they initiated in the void, with a decent obligation to explain everything to mankind but no formal obligation to anything or anybody. Twenty-five years later, Jefferson's First Inaugural breathes exactly the same spirit, only more so. In the changed circumstances, it is personal, offhand, self-assured, like the remarks of a professor who has been elected temporary rector by his own faculty. No aura attaches to the Presidency. To be political, to govern, is an ordinary human act. (John Adams had tried to work up a little aura, and Jefferson didn't like it.)

In this view, political institutions are nothing but deliberate social experiments. In a beautiful passage, Madison explains the advantages of decentralism: each autonomous unit can experiment; if the experiment fails, only a small community is hurt, and the others can help out; if the experiment succeeds, it can be imitated to everybody's advantage. (It *is* a misfortune that the Federal system of States has not operated in this way. I can think of only a few radical experiments, in Minnesota, Wisconsin, Louisiana. If Upton Sinclair's EPIC program in California had come to power, it might have been the most interesting.)

To cement this easy assumption of a band of citizens who could experiment on their own and give mutual support, there were, of course, shared assumptions in moral philosophy and on the Nature of Man. There was an acceptance of human diversity, but a confidence, as is clear in *The Federalist*, that there need never be party divisions, though there would undoubtedly be "factions." Common reason, a common ultimate goal would provide coherence.

More deeply, people used to autonomy experienced no conflict between reason and feeling, or between objectivity and engagement. This led to a crucially important view of history, that existing conditions were *plastic* to human purposes. Problems were amenable to improvement by practical proposals, and these practical proposals would be put into effect by the meeting of minds. Typically, Washington and his friends were great canal planners. (Some of the canals, like the Ohio-Potomac, were never dug.) By the same token, past history was assiduously studied because of its moral lessons, as a source of examples for present action.

In this idyllic climate there was no thought of powerlessness and very little thought of coercion. Historical conditions were *for* men to act in, and men *could* act. So far as centralization and top-down direction were necessary, they were built into the system in a characteristic style: federation, limited sovereignty, multifarious checks and balances. The very calling of a constitutional convention, for example, implied that others could and would be called—perhaps "every twenty years," so that each generation could again make society. There is no rhetoric that "what we now do will last a thousand years."

The checks and balances are regarded by historians as compromises, between big States and small States, between monarchic Executive and popular Legislature, etc.; and of course, so they were. But more importantly, they expressed a positive theory about Human Nature: that each man is fired by special interests and is cooperative; he is reflective and executive; he is initiating and obedient to Law; he is conservative and progressive; he is individualistic and social. Naturally, in these polarities, some men or groups would opt strongly for one or another extreme, but these would constitute only transient factions.

6

As the country passed into the Jacksonian period, however, the face-to-face structured groups were steadily disrupted. Master-apprentice and indenture relations gave way first to paternal capitalism and then to the formation of a proletariat. With new technology, family-slavery and gentry-farming rapidly became field-slavery on big plantations. With the growth of urban population, there was cash-cropping on an increased scale. There was an increase of absentee ownership and abstract money, banking, and investment.

In this disruption, the more powerful persons could combine in new functional associations, whether joint-stock corporations or lobbies, forming new centers. But the smaller people tended to become homogenized. The new immigrants, *e.g.* Negro or Irish, were "mere" labor.

There then began to be a sense of impersonal "objective" conditions. In the utilitarian mode, the rhetoric began to abound in statistics and in enthusiastic identification with rather abstract national goals and achievement, such as growth of population, territory, and wealth, and also with being part of a mighty interlocking system of division of labor, both craft and sectional. (Of course this rhetoric was largely true; the question is, Under what conditions are people moved by it?) With the imposition of tariffs, manipulated currency, the terms of admission of new States, and pork-barreling public works, people now had a vital stake in centralized politics and the community-anarchy was at an end. The more homogenized majority was able to force a nearly universal white adult male suffrage.

In the new abstract relations, there were irreconcilable conflicts, not to be settled by practical proposals meeting common agreement: class conflict, conflict of sections, conflict of city and country. Factions became permanent parties, looking for mass support in the wide suffrage, and the sense of history was entirely transformed. History was now an It that had to be pushed; it was the tendency of objective conditions which could be influenced to one's advantage by belonging to the victorious Party and sharing in the spoils. Correspondingly, compromise was no longer a reasoned positive solution but an avoidance of worse conflict. But nothing could really be settled.

Naturally, the division into only two mass parties, necessary to try to gain the upper hand, could not represent the actual manifold conflicts of interest. The more "popular" party might represent small debt-ridden farmers and urban workingmen, but it might also represent the country against the city, the South against the North. The more elite party might represent Industry and therefore urban jobs, but also rural stability and gentry. Inevitably, political rhetoric became blurred and phony, and the patriotic rhetoric of cohesiveness tended to become symbolic and emotional, abounding in "our heritage" and in panegyric that the continent was broad.

Fatefully, government itself became an independent institution of society, rather than an existential act of ordinary citizens. Men "ran for office" as once the office had sought the man. The change in the attitude toward the Constitution is significant. There began to be a pedantry and aura of the text. It was no longer regarded as a man-made document that might be remade—though in fact it was continually being remade, *e.g.* by the Party system itself.

Government, especially the Presidency, assumed the curious dual role that we are used to. On the one hand, it was the victorious Party with a drive toward tyranny of the majority. But on the other, it was an impersonal arbiter among the irreconcilable conflicting groups. (Jackson: "There are no necessary evils in government. If it would confine itself to equal protection and shower its favors alike on the high and the low, it would be an unqualified blessing." Note that this was still the opinion of the popular Party, not the plutocrats.)

Finally, by the familiar psychological mechanism, with the increase of powerlessness, internal tension, and sectionalism, there developed xenophobia and narrow patriotism, instead of the beautiful Enlightenment tolerance and internationalism of the preceding generation. The universal ideal of education of Jefferson and Madison lapsed into sectarian and elite colleges. The electorate divided into ethnic and religious blocs.

On the other hand, of course, it was an open society, with opportunity and space, and there were strong forces toward both community and personal freedom. There was the possibility, in some places transiently realized, of combining industrial and farm occupations, for no enclosures threw the farmers off the land. The combination could be capitalistic, as when textile mills hired surplus farm girls, or it could be communal, as in the Owenite or Fourierist experiments.

It is during this period that Tocqueville speaks with admiration of the disposition of Americans to form voluntary associations to perform every kind of function. But unfortunately, just those associations which might essentially have countervailed the new homogenizing conditions, e.g. craft unions and the intentional communities, proved abortive. Indeed, in some respects the freedom of the frontier and the expansion of wealth were misfortunes, since they provided easy safety valves. And the immigration provided industrial labor that was exploitable in a way that prosperous yeomen were not. Perhaps just at this time, at the beginning of modern industrial society, people with the original American character could have hammered out authentic institutions.

As it was, moral philosophy fell apart into three kinds of theories: Calhoun's "types of mankind," with irreconcilable interests and the need for a balancing strong authority; the egalitarianism without qualities that Tocqueville complains of; and the individualism of Emerson and Thoreau. This last is terribly prescient of the generations to come, when civilized society is regarded as coercive and corrupt, when the consensus is always in the wrong, and when a man must break away into the physical or moral wilderness in order to be free and noble.

7

The outcry of Populism marked the crisis in the feeling of loss of power, which is our theme. More than the beginnings of the modern labor movement during the same period, and certainly more than Reform politics, Populism clearly saw the closing trap of interlocking centralization. Like any war, the Civil War had centralized and overcapitalized. Now the free market was restrained by trusts and ever higher tariffs. As producers and consumers, the farmers were squeezed by railroads, packers, manufacturers. There were new immigration and accelerated urbanization. The political parties became entirely massified and distantly controlled, and there were alliances between government and the monopolies. To all this, the Populists responded with heroic self-reliance, and tragic paranoia and political confusion.

In my opinion, this was the last American political movement to face squarely the crucial dilemma of modern society: how to preserve practical democracy in high industrial conditions. For a couple of decades, Populism saw the answer: the Jacksonian Party democracy could not work; one had to start anew from below.

Inevitably, but unfortunately, the movement was agrarian, since only the farmers had a live sense of the practical independence they were losing. From its beginnings, the American workingmen's movement had accepted the role assigned to it by management, of being wage-slaves, and its demands were merely for shorter hours, higher pay, and safer and more dignified conditions; it was not syndicalist, seeking power, and it was not anarchist, seeking workers' management. To the extent that the labor movement was political, it looked to socialist collectivism, with top-down administration, though without competition and profits.

The rhetoric of Populism was apocalyptic; people were trapped in the Last Times. Let me cull from the Platform of 1892: "Our country finds itself confronted by conditions for which there is no precedent in the history of the world. . . . A vast conspiracy against mankind has been organized and is rapidly taking possession of the world. If not met and overthrown at once, it forebodes terrible social convulsions, the destruction of civilization. . . . These are the issues upon which not only our individual prosperity but the very existence of free institutions depend." Strikingly —*e.g.* in the Declaration of the National Grange, 1874 —the Constitutional appeal now went back to the Preamble, for all the rest had become suspect. Yet this rhetoric was not, in the end, exaggerated, for since that period the older democracy has indeed been dead, and the national States have mounted two world wars and have a thousand overkill in nuclear bombs.

8

With the Apocalypse, there was an efflorescence of
paranoia, especially in the form of suspicion of all
strangers, who were the troops of the diabolic entrapment. Absentee owners were all Jews. Cheap immi-
grant labor was part of the plot. For a brief spell, Negroes were equally oppressed brothers, but very soon
they became diabolically black. The East consisted of
Cities of Sin; it poisoned the food with preservatives
and made shoddy and obsolescent manufactures to bilk
the honest. Following out the logic, it was necessary to
complete a North-South waterway—in principle the
St. Lawrence Seaway connected with the Mississippi
and the Gulf of Mexico—to by-pass the East altogether
in overseas trade, and exclude it from the national
economy!

Government, too, was part of the entrapment. Politics was dirty in its nature and no honest man would
seek office. Like the labor movement of the same period, the Populists continually disclaimed the revolutionary politics that were implicit in their protest. Yet,
at the same time, they clamored for nationalization of
the railroads and utilities and some industries, for
strengthening the civil service, for establishment of the
Federal regulatory agencies, and for a graduated income tax to be dispensed from Washington. *These* demands became, of course, the platform of the lapse of
Populism into Progressivism and modern Liberalism.

9

The relations between Populism and the labor
movement were tragically askew, so that at this critical
moment again it was impossible to form a united and
successful movement to ease us into the twentieth century. The groups respected each other and expressed

sympathy, but they could not cooperate. First, there was a superficial clash of interests, the workers in manufacturing and transport wanting higher wages and the farmers cheaper goods. More deeply, the farmers tended to include all urban workers in the hated circle of foreigners and people dependent and lackeys by nature. Also, though they believed fervently in cooperation, the Populist cooperatives did not resist using their own enterprises to gouge profits whenever they could, and this was contradictory to the truer socialism of the more extreme labor movement.

On the other hand, the labor movement was persistently wrong in principle. As it was set up, it could not be an instrument to struggle against the enclosing trap —and indeed we see, a half century later, that either in its bureaucratized or in its Statist form, labor-unionism has become a chief partner in centralization.

In Europe there had been a sharp conflict in unionism, between the centralizing Marxist and welfare-statists and the decentralizing Proudhonists, Bakuninists, and Guild Socialists. Fundamentally, the decentralists wanted worker-management in one form or other. Their workers tended to belong especially to highly skilled, self-reliant, or daring occupations— watchmakers, artist-craftsmen, peasants, miners, lumbermen, seamen—and they felt that they could manage handsomely without top-down direction. They looked to a future of syndicalist federation as the organization of society.* The Marxist and La Sallean unions, on the

* It is interesting to notice, also, the humanistic and, so to speak, ecological background of the anarchist leaders. Kropotkin was a geographer and agronomist, E. Reclus was a geographer, Fanelli an architect, Pelloutier a lawyer specializing in labor and civil liberties, Malatesta had studied medicine, Morris was an arts-and-craftsman, Ferrer was a progressive educator. All this was very different from being an economist, politician-lawyer, academic, or technologist.

other hand, worked at routinized occupations in highly rationalized plants; they formed bureaucratic and centralized parties; and they looked to a future of top-down planning and administration. In my opinion, it was a disaster that this tendency (which was in the minority) gained control of the international labor movement, for the decentralist guilds and syndical federations would have countervailed the subsequent overcentralization.

It is possible—to make a pointless speculation—that in America a more daring labor theory, concentrating factory, might have been more congenial to Populism. and Emerson: the idea of humanizing industrialism and Certainly the most "anarchist" American labor organization, the IWW, did best on Populist soil. As it was, however, the Populists looked askance at the foreign socialists—intellectual Germans and Jews who had fled Europe in 1849 or from the Czar. Meantime, like the Populists themselves, the skilled craft-unionists sought their own short-range interest.

10

Despite paranoia, pettiness, and political confusion, the effort of the Populists is beyond praise, to reopen society, starting at the bottom, by the process of Do-It-Yourself. They excellently analyzed the costs of distribution and how to diminish them, the dangers of one-crop farming, the need to avoid "the credit system, the mortgage system, the fashion system," and how to substitute their own arbitration for litigation. In political theory, they pushed to abolish the Party system, for direct primaries, and popular initiative and referendum. These were consistent with their best inspiration, and are probably necessary for any modern workable democracy. (Of themselves, of course, they guarantee nothing.) With amazing cooperativeness and energy, each farm stringing its wire, they built their own phone systems, and even managed to construct short railroad lines. Their merchandising cooperatives saved them 40 and 50 per cent. They organized their own insurance.

With this went an emphasis on universal education of the practical kind. Populism inspired the best vocational high schools, the flowering of the land-grant colleges, and adult education. My feeling is that the functionalism of Sullivan and Wright, the pragmatic sociology of Mead and Veblen, and the progressive education of Dewey were nourished by the climate of Populism more than by the labor movement. They constitute the specifically American contribution to world philosophy, following and perfecting Jefferson and Emerson: the idea of humanizing industrialism and re-establishing community democracy among alienated and powerless masses.

11

Lapsing into Progressivism, Liberal Democracy, and the New Deal, the programs of Populism, the labor movement, and Debs socialism have, for the most part, become the law of the land; but in their effect they have been entirely transformed by becoming bureaucratized and administered from above. It is a remarkable proof, if proof were needed, that the method is more important than the content. These programs were designed to strengthen the hand of independent groups; they have succeeded in centrally organizing society more tightly and more in depth. Each step of the way —primaries, referendum, regulatory agencies, increasing the years of compulsory schooling, progressive income tax, muckraking, women's suffrage, right to organize, minimum wage, social security, etc., etc.— promised to be a revolutionary democratizing of society, and was so attacked and so championed. Yet all have cumulatively added up to the one interlocked system of big government, big corporations, big municipalities, big labor, big education, and big communications, in which all of us are pretty regimented and brainwashed, and in which direct initiative and deciding have become difficult or impossible.

In the past ten or fifteen years, especially during the Eisenhower and Kennedy Administrations, this *fait accompli* of centralization has dawned on the general consciousness. It has been the theme of dozens of books of social criticism. Yet the response to it has been entirely different from the apocalyptic frenzy of the Populists when the trap was closing. The present belief is that "under modern conditions," the trap is inevitable and we are powerless. This sentiment is itself an effect of accustomed powerlessness. One can no longer even imagine another state, not to speak of inventing means to it and trying to execute them.

What is the objective background? During the twentieth century, we have engaged in two world wars. It is said that Wilson hesitated to enter World War I because it would be necessary to subsidize corporations that would never cut back. He was right. The United States is now the chief imperialist power, with a vast permanent military and overcapitalized industries to support the role. The warring trusts have settled into a system of semi-monopolies, with fixed prices, for mutual security. The free market has turned into a synthetic creature of advertising. Government has entered into colossal alliances: in real estate, with municipalities and promoters; in agriculture, with giant croppers and grocery chains; in science and education, with the universities and high-technology corporations; in highways, with automomile manufacturers and oil men.

A sovereign citizenry is no longer even thought of. Let me quote two remarks of Franklin Roosevelt: "The day of the Politician is past; the day of the Enlightened Administrator has come"—the State had already withered away!—"The greatest duty of a statesman is to educate." What a remarkable change in American theory! Madison thought that it was the democratic process itself that educated. But for Roosevelt there is an ongoing system expertly tended by administrators, and there is a mass of pupils who do not know how to fend for themselves—especially the "underprivileged." There have ceased to be prudent or angry citizens.

Since the New Deal paternalism, we have seen two strikingly different images of administration, Eisenhower's non-intervention and Kennedy's let's-get-a-move-on, yet social changes have had little to do with these differences. Automation, urbanization, Negro revolution, colonial revolution have developed according to their own laws. Government policy, so far as there is policy, resides mainly in the entrenched system of the Civil Service, Pentagon, Scientific Foundations, and proliferating Agencies that are hardly subject to political decision. There has been a great addition of school-monks, but they have been nicely organized into the same structure. All this grinds on, not incompetently, not without benevolence, and with surprisingly little peculation. (Significantly, it is only the secret, para-political agencies, FBI and CIA, that seem dangerous, because they *might* do something unforeseen.)

This machine runs, by and large, for its own sake. The real form of sovereignty is democracy-by-consent, with a post-political unanimity on the issues that are inherent in the system itself: the expanding GNP, the Cold War, the solution of problems by adding new agencies staffed by school-monks. Occasional moments of living politics occur when some condition becomes intolerable and there is an outcry. The political solution is to try to make it not intolerable by money, a new agency, or at least a commission of inquiry. Embarrassing or dissenting officials may be shifted to other departments; the seasoned never quit and nobody is fired.

It is said that governmental power has all gravitated to the Executive, away from the Congress who, like people, can only consent or balk. Extreme liberals are now hot to streamline Congress so it cannot even balk. But in the system we have been describing, the Executive also is not a governing person nor group of persons, any more than the baronial corporations are persons except as a fiction. During the activist Kennedy regime, frustration was continually expressed because, somehow, the Cabinet and the President himself were powerless. Just so the heads of giant corporations and of apparently autonomous universities claim that they are powerless to alter policies that they say they disapprove of. It is inherent in centralization that powerlessness spreads from the bottom to the top. There is certainly a structure of power in the country, but it seems to be a misnomer to call it a power *elite*.

It has become common to call this mighty interlocking organization the Establishment, usually with an ironical but comfortable satisfaction, as if America had come of age. This conception is ludicrous. The cultural baseness of the executives, whether in government, the universities, or broadcasting; the communal moronism of the city and regional planners; the qualitative deterioration of the standard of living; the frantic insecurity of the middle class; the reduction of the authority of Law to force—such things are the contrary of Establishment. The idea of an Establishment is

to provide a tolerable setting in which the serious
affairs of life can proceed unhampered, spontaneously,
often eccentrically, within agreed limits of style. Instead, not unlike a garrison state, our organization invades, and dispirits, every detail of life; it discourages
dissent and kills spontaneity. It does have a style—I
myself fall into it—but I do not think I agree.

When people feel powerless, they no longer think
there is practicable history. "Pragmatic," as used for
instance by the Kennedy regime, comes to mean keeping the works going, without a goal outside itself, and
finally without information outside itself. So, in both
domestic and foreign affairs, history and policy consist
of coping with unanticipated events, almost on a day-
to-day basis. Here is a typical anecdote to illustrate
what I mean: There was a crisis in Panama set off by a
petty incident in a seething environment. Out of the
files at the State Department came an accurate predic-
tion of the very event, made six years before, and ad-
vising remedies; but of course at *that* time it was not
"pragmatic" to act, for Panama was not part of the
day's news that realistic politicians cope with. It was
now too late to act on the good advice.

This is the political reality in which occur the para-
legal movements mentioned in the preceding chapter.

12

We thus come out with the paradoxes that we have
sought to explain. The gentlemen of the Right, who
invented the protective tariff and the trusts, now complain in Populist terms that liberty is encroached on.
But liberal democrats, the old champions of *laissez
faire*, come on like pillars of the Establishment, patrons
of monasteries, and almsgivers to the poor, as if they
were royalists. *They* have the responsibility to keep

the show going. As Mr. Schlesinger put it, "One simply must govern."

Middle-class citizens withdraw from civic responsibility into suburban privacy, and leave the central city to segregation and blight. But poor Negroes and Puerto Ricans, bearded students, and Bohemian artists exercise citizenly initiative and engage in reform politics.

CHAPTER III

Some Baronial Domains

1

It is a slogan of the Right that the evils of central power can be avoided by restoring many functions to the municipalities, the States, and something called private enterprise. So in this chapter let us look at a little assortment of non-Federal systems. It is puzzling, however, what is meant by "private" enterprise, since the corporations referred to are controlled not by their stockholders but by proxies, like any other democracy-by-consent; they pre-empt the means of production and therefore control producers; and as semi-monopolies or monopolies they fix prices and therefore exact taxes on the general public. The only plausible description of them is feudal domains.

2

We can regard the New York City school system as an example of a classical bureaucracy. (Let me say that I have an affection for this system, of which I am a product. It is earnestly democratic and rather warmly concerned for children, rather than business, prestige, or brainwashing like some other school systems. Its defects are absolute, but they come from trying to do a job that is impossible by the methods employed.)

The system serves a million children. There are 750 schools rather rigidly controlled by one headquarters. The annual budget exceeds $700,000,000, excluding capital costs. About fifteen new schools or replacements are budgeted every year, at a cost of from $2,500,000 to $5,000,000 each. There are more than 60,000 employees, including 44,000 teachers.

The structure of this vast enterprise has been little changed from an ancient plan, but simply aggrandized, though conditions have utterly changed. For instance, in 1900 only 6 per cent of the seventeen-year-olds graduated from high school, now more than 60 per cent, and during this period the ethnic and class composition and, of course, the educational needs of the children have wildly varied. Yet the institution has not altered except by adding on new services and departments. Anyway, since public schooling is so acutely sensitive to know-nothing indignation by church, press, and politicians, any radical experiment in plant, methods, or instruction would be out of the question. At present, in my opinion, this structure is so fundamentally out of touch that it has ceased to educate at all, though it preserves the name of a system of Education.

There are the expected hang-ups due to mere bureaucratic size. Here are actual situations. To remove a door catch that hampers the use of a lavatory requires a long appeal through headquarters, because it is "city property." A principal cannot call an exterminator to get rid of rats, but there must be picketing by parents to force a visit by the Mayor so that he can exterminate. I mentioned above the establishment of new local boards with indeterminate powers: after a year of operation, the coordinator of these boards at headquarters explained to us that their main achievement so far had been to make it possible for the field superintendents to communicate with headquarters, through the mediation of persistent local board members. For instance, a valuable new press had been given to the High School of Printing, and it was necessary to remove a wall in order to install it; but this required a rubber stamp from an Associate Superintendent. The donor of the press had agreed to cover all costs. Yet after two years and a mountain of correspondence, the rubber stamp was still not forthcoming. A local board pounded a table and got it in two days.

Despite bureaucratic pedantry, there is the expected peculation. An old-fashioned type of hardware is specified for all new buildings, that is kept in production only for the New York school system. Janitors have been taking home $50,000 a year. It costs several hundred thousand dollars to fix a roof that still leaks. On the other hand, there is public uproar because of trivialities or nothing: a high school student has carpentered a boat for a school official.

In the standard procedure, the purpose of the enterprise is lost sight of. An architect is not "allowed" to consult the teachers or principal of a school that he is replacing, because he must follow standard plans that are a generation out of date. For specific pedagogic purposes, a principal asks for soundproofing, but this is not standard and cannot be specified. A district has 35 per cent Puerto Ricans who cannot speak English, but it is impossible to get bilingual teachers, for there is a rule that teachers must have no trace of a foreign accent. (This rule has been modified.) Instead, applicants for teacher in New York City spend months or years learning a peculiar "correct" pronunciation that is heard nowhere else on land or sea. To process teacher applications takes nearly a year, so that excellent young people choose rather to apply in the suburbs, where the salary is similar and the work easier. Yet in such a vast system, it *is* necessary to be meticulous about due process, to avoid injustice, political pressure, and nepotism.

The teachers have succeeded in organizing a strong union. Many, perhaps most, of the teachers are dedicated professionals and are mainly concerned about professional problems, especially diminishing class size and having a say in curriculum and methods. But the union, mesmerized by the abstract theory of the laboring class, can strike only for wages and definite schedules, *e.g.* no extracurricular duties. This dispirits the members.

Having lost touch with its function and philosophy, the school system has to cope by improvisations with external real social problems for which it is not prepared, and with public fads which it cannot simply brush off—Negro revolution, dropouts, sputnik, audio-visual technology, why-Johnny-can't-read. Inevitably, it resorts to the usual liberal Tokenism. It puffs a new program into a big deal for public relations, does not seriously implement it or demand enough money for it, and absorbs it into the hoary structure in which nothing can change. I have heard the system described as a torpid dinosaur in a cold swamp; one lights a fire under her but produces very little motion; and she soon settles back.

A new program might in itself be a good one, *e.g.* to expose underprivileged children to more of the middle-class environment; but it will be diluted and standardized into routine tours or going to *West Side Story* (! —one would have thought that this play was a

Broadway effort to expose overprivileged adults to more of the underprivileged environment). An extremely relevant program to bring competent adults into the schools to give the children some attention is trivialized by jealousy about professional perquisites. The Parent-Teacher Associations are reduced to a pressure group on Albany.

There is the usual incredible face-saving. For instance, in answering a recent questionnaire on violence in the schools, more than 20 per cent of parents and more than 20 per cent of teachers said that they knew, personally or by direct hearsay, of violent incidents; yet all but one per cent of supervisors denied that any such things existed. And timidity and face-saving go down the chain of command. Many a stormy and even dangerous case of discipline arises for no other reason than that a teacher is afraid that the supervisor will walk in and see a child chewing gum. There is a passionate attempt to maintain an unearthly quiet.

With so much supervision, shifting of responsibility, jealous defense of role and perquisites, snowfalls of paperwork, and difficulties of communication, extra personnel proliferate. There is forever need of new assistant principals, clerks, secretaries, guidance counselors, experts in remedial reading, truant officers, school aides. This runs into big money, yet the fundamental pedagogic fact of overcrowded classes cannot be altered because of expense and lack of space. For putative efficiencies, each school building is made too large. An intelligent principal asks for a maximum of four hundred children—so he can know each child's name —but some schools have eighteen hundred. Finally, an official limit of twelve hundred is decreed; then Negro parents, egged on by Reform politicians, balk at this as an attempt to deprive their children of the new building. The requirements of the educational community are invariably sacrificed to administrative convenience, ignorant public pressure, and false economy.

All this, however, is at present only the beginning of the strains on this system. For now it is being increasingly tightly interlocked with the other aggrandizing systems of school and society on a national scale. The curriculum is trapped by endless national testing and fierce competition for the colleges, which in turn are geared to graduate schools and scientific corporations. The textbook manufacturers and manufacturers of teaching machines are crowding in. National Educational Television has entered the system—with typical abstract virtue and concrete disaster: in principle TV should be a vivid aid, but the educational variety is dull as illustration because the school system can take no chances, and it is a waste of time in the classroom because it intrudes between teacher and pupils. Earnest prospective teachers used to run the obstacle course of only graduate schools of education, but now they have to satisfy the National Science Foundation as well. The school system must suddenly meet—or pretend to meet—the needs of the Expanding Economy, the Cold War, Unemployment, Urban Delinquency. This leaves not much leeway for educating children, even if the system could.

But to illustrate the effects of external interlocking, let us turn to another kind of enterprise.

3

In the case of the schools, the internal organization prevents the function, educating. In the case of the manufacture of cars, the internal organization has no doubt facilitated the "function," making money. But the aggrandizement of the centralized complex of marketing, servicing, and highway construction has led to such an overgrowth that a useful industry has turned into a menace. It has transformed the entire environment in unforeseen ways and has ended up by dictating a whole way of life.

During the twenties, automobiles began to be sold for style and status rather than convenience and serious use. Meantime a developing suburban middle class pushed, at general expense, for the construction of the parkways. Over the years, largely pointless annual model changes and high-powered advertising have created a synthetic demand and removed natural limitations on the proliferation of such formidable and expensive objects. (A couple of hundred dollars per car is added for the annual model change.) There is now a car for every 2.7 Americans, much more than one to a family, and every effort is made to increase the number.

Highways are built at a cost varying from a half million to three million dollars a mile. (For example, the Garden State Parkway, 173 miles for $370,000,000. Or, a six-mile stretch from Yonkers to Pelham is estimated to cost $25,000,000 to *re*build, presumably without cost for right-of-way.) After armaments, highway construction is the big item in Federal budgets, and it looms immensely in State budgets. It is estimated that by 1970 a single one-way five-mile trip to the center of Washington will have cost $2.50 per car per trip for the roadway. This is not a very efficient means of mass transportation! Again, more than 50 per cent of the area of downtown Los Angeles is now occupied by roads and parkways.

This complex of cars, oil, and roads looms so large in the national economy that a falling off in car sales can precipitate a serious recession. General Motors' sales are over $12,000,000,000 annually; Standard Oil over $9,000,000,000. General Motors alone employs 600,000 people. Charles Wilson's remark, "What is good for

General Motors is good for the country," was a serious one. Another way of saying it is that the automotive complex can now exercise a blackmail to dictate further development in public works, regional planning, and the pattern of urban and suburban life. Typically, at the 1964 meeting of the nation's highway planners, the Federal government was urged to speed up and blueprint its housing program, so that the highways could be laid down, for "any interruption in the highway improvement program can have serious adverse effects on the national economy." One would normally think of transportation as getting from place to place; we are now to think of places as terminals of transportation. And of transportation as a means to increase the sale of cars and rationalize the improvement of highways.

Similarly, in the current style of urbanism, the precondition of any plan is the highway pattern. If congestion becomes intolerable, the remedy is to narrow sidewalks, cut down trees, displace tenants and tradesmen. There is never a thought of banning the cars from the center or planning to diminish traffic.

Because of direct and indirect subsidy, the cars and trucks have been pushing other kinds of transportation out of the picture. Until the last couple of years, there has not even been thought of a balanced transit, using all technical means to serve the general convenience. For instance, eighty lanes of highways are necessary for the traffic that could be carried on two tracks of rails. The fleets of cars on suburban parkways make no economic or psychological sense, and the congestion is often intolerable. (However, a new computer system has just been devised at M. I. T. that will drive your car along the parkways for you and presumably speed things up. "Despite the convenience of rapid transit," explains Professor Robert Mann, "everybody likes to drive his own car.") In most large cities, the problems of traffic and parking are out of hand. And the dangerous new artifact of urban smog is directly traceable to the cars; with a temporary banning of cars in Manhattan, there was a 66 per cent reduction of air pollution in two days.

Three or four manufacturers control the automobile market, competing with fixed prices and slowly spooned-out improvements. Apparently, General Motors could pre-empt the entire market but chooses the semi-monopolistic situation either as better sales rhetoric, or to avoid regulation as a monopoly, or for other reasons unknown to me. Over the years, progress in design has been determined entirely to maximize profits, rather than to reduce price or improve the product. For instance, air conditioning has been withheld for forty years. Smog control is scandalously in abeyance. The recent seller has been increased power, which is unfunctional for most situations. There is evidence that even safety is not a crucial consideration; the only crucial consideration is sales to increasingly ignorant consumers through increasingly ignorant dealers. In 1964, 47,000 were killed in automobile accidents, an increase of 8 per cent over 1963. Auto theft has become the chief felony, overwhelmingly for juveniles—and this is, importantly I think, because of the nature of the advertising.

Radically new design is impossible, for, even with good intentions, the groups controlling a market will advance according to their own expertness, patents, and previous tooling, and will pay no attention to other directions. Only the competition of European small cars made a difference, for a time. I do not know of any effort to develop an efficient, slower moving electric for urban use (especially taxis).

Expensive as they are, cars are built not to last. The

manufacturers push for laws exempting them from supplying replacement parts for more than five years. Also, whether deliberately or carelessly, there seems to be no effort to make the machines more comprehensible and repairable by users. The tendency has been uniformly in the opposite direction, to make the users increasingly dependent on the increasingly centralized nexus of sales and service.

Of course, it is a matter of opinion whether the actual improvements in speed, manner of operation, appliances, and cosmetics have warranted the continual scrapping and the expense of the model changes. (For twenty-five years, I myself, for various reasons, have found myself happy driving cars five to ten years behind the current model. My '53 Chevy has not obsolesced. Advt.) Certainly the procedure is the opposite of the original plan of Henry Ford, to arrive at a good model and sell it cheap. And it seems odd to merchandise such remarkable machines in terms of fads and fashions, as if they were ladies' dresses.

Meantime, as a neglected but fatal consequence of the colossal aggrandizement of this one complex, primarily for profit and only secondarily for use, there has been imposed an entirely new and disruptive plan on every community. Suburbanization and urban sprawl were not started by the cars, but in their virulent form they are largely creatures of the cars. Villages and city neighborhoods have been disrupted by highway shopping centers. In industry, because of the cars, there have sprung up vast concentrations of plant, and, in education, central schools, claiming enhanced efficiency because of the concentration; but the hidden costs of highways, cars, fuel, and commuting are never counted in the cost of production, and only partly in the school budget. Instead of developing integrated neighborhoods of residence, work, culture, and recrea-

tion, we have bought into a style of dispersal dependent on automobility. This will soon come to total
frustration when, because of congestion, the cars cease
to move.

Thus, an industry that developed because of reasonable choices of real advantages has become, by hypertrophy and systematic expansion, an ineluctable deter-
minant. And now, fascinatingly, a billion dollars are
asked for redevelopment of the depressed area of Appalachia, and of this sum $840,000,000 are for a highway
system—to which the States will add $360,000,000, mak-
ing $1.2 billion for the roads! By contrast, $220,000,000
will be spent for "improved health facilities, timber
development, water resources, reclamation of aban-
doned mines, vocational education, improved sewage,
and other Federal grants-in-aid."

My argument is simple. A more decentralized and
varied development, less dominated by an overwhelming central combination, would have allowed other
community forces to assert themselves and countervail, achieving a better balance of means and a more
organic adjustment to technological advances. I think
this example is representative of our technological
"progress" in general. (Consider the complex of sky-
scraper construction and real-estate speculation as analogous.)

In the mess we are in, however, I can see no remedy
but authoritarian public planning to express further
community needs than making profits for automobile
manufacturers.

4

When we turn to the interlocking systems of mass
communications, with very few men at the top, the
public danger is obvious—brainwashing—and prudent
critics keep pointing it out. The danger is at the level

of a constitutional crisis, for with brainwashing even democracy-by-consent becomes impossible. Yet there is almost no thought of a remedy, not to speak of public action. (I propose a remedy in Appendix VI.)

Fewer than sixty cities have competing newspapers —in 1900 there were six hundred. These papers are served by two or three international news services. Three big broadcasting networks get most of their news from the same sources, playing up the pictorial aspects of topics that have already been judged as the "news." Yet, with the best will in the world and the highest standards of impartial journalism, so few minds responsible for decision cannot possibly know what *is* the important news. To give a current example, isn't it remarkable that the underground take-over of the Republican Party by the forces behind Goldwater was so little reported from 1959-64? But it was not yet "news." (Contrast "engaged editing," as described in Appendix VII.)

The right balance of control of mass communications is a difficult problem. To provide a day-to-day international news service does require an immense centralized organization. There are standard services and occasional ceremonial or exciting events that can admirably be covered by national TV at great expense —major sports, the report of the moon rocket, political conventions. (For instance, the rights to televise a championship football game cost $1,800,000. But I fail to see how things like the election coverage, for instance, are a *news* service. I think that the public would find out anyway who was elected President, even if the computer did not make its guesses.) Yet only a mixed system, of central standard communications and *very* many decentralized but widely heard communications, can give adequate information. As it is, the majority of people—and even the Central Intel-

ligence Agency—are often surprised by events that
tiny newsletters have been following and confidently
predicting.

The situation is not helped by official press releases
that pass for news and by tit-for-tat arrangements:
print my press release and I'll let you in on some real
news.

The dissemination of opinion is equally restricted.
On reasonable commercial grounds, the TV networks
have pushed through the revocation of equal time for
all parties in national campaigns and are seeking the
same for State campaigns. There is no reason, says Mr.
Stanton of CBS, to broadcast to a general public the
quixotic views of splinter groups. This means that Fré-
mont, the first Republican candidate, would not have
had the media in 1856, though Lincoln carried in 1860.
And we have seen that the bulk of the Socialist program of 1912 is now the law of the land, including
conservation, workmen's compensation, and the forty-
eight-hour week.

Since there are limited channels for broadcasting, if
the networks control most of the licensees, there is an
implicit censorship. And often enough the censorship
has become explicit. Certain speakers are overtly or
tacitly blacklisted. Tapes are wiped out as too controversial—*e.g.* a rational colloquium on the Sexual Revolution was wiped out of *Open End*. The FCC has
proved powerless to compel "reasonable coverage."
And though the channels are public property, the licenses seem to be given in perpetuity.

The networks wield enormous potential political
power. In one instance, a network was able overnight
to muster ten thousand telegrams to Congress from
children, because the bad regulatory agency was, by its
policy, threatening to do away with a popular dog
program.

The Standard of Living—how it is decent to live—
and what is correct in style and in entertainment are
determined by these same networks interlocked with a
few national magazines. Both these groups are "sus-
tained" by the same advertisers. The system of commercial sponsorship requires creating and maintaining
a mass audience, and the accepted technique is to combine the sensational with the inoffensive. Anything
that might displease a large segment, a few hundred
thousand out of many millions, cannot be shown. By
law, the sponsors are not supposed to influence programming, which is the responsibility of the licensee;
but of course big corporations that pay for big shows
(the NBC national hook-up costs $140,000 an hour)
reasonably want what is dignified or otherwise appropriate to their image. The storm of angry letters that is
dreaded by sponsors might be as few as twenty; this
number will then have a definite influence on what can
be communicated to the American people. This is another striking illustration of the powerlessness of apparently powerful central decision-makers, just as
wardens are jailed by inmates. The audience cannot be
given better fare and the broadcasters do not dare to
give it; then the broadcasters conclude that "the audience gets what it wants." It is certain that no human
animal is really satisfied by this porridge. As the British
Pilkington Report on Television has pointed out,
every person has authentic interests and tastes,
whether in gardening, mathematical puzzles, or arche-
ology, but each such group will number at most a few
hundred thousand; except for major events or national
politics, there are no authentic groups in the multimil-
lions.

By the same token, the effect of advertising on me-
dium-size national magazines, say up to a million circulation, is much less virulent. Within broad limits, such

magazines can print anything that will attract the circulation that determines their advertising rates; they do not need to cling to "everybody." (As a writer, however—my essays are occasionally usable in the category of conversation pieces—I am not altogether happy with being part of the "non-sustaining" department of these magazines. It was not for this that Sam Johnson and Fleet Street broke the patronage system and brought together the writer and the public.) But with the really big audiences, say five million, experience has been showing that nothing that magazines can venture, in the sensational or the bland, can avail against TV pictures, and these magazines lose their advertisers.

The most disastrous effect of the giant commercial system is not in content but in form. In broadcasting, the expensive time is cut for sale like bolts of cloth, it demands minute-and-second scheduling, and this has created a format of regimented panel discussions, twelve-minute vignettes, episodic plots interruptible for the ad, in which any spontaneity or thoroughness of expression is out of the question. And the miracle of the TV medium itself—the old dream of seeing at a distance—is sacrificed. Unrehearsed reality must be avoided or used only in edited tapes, for any particular stretch that an advertiser has bought is likely to be boring or, during it, something untoward might occur. The TV disposition to format can serve us as a model of overcentralization: how to take the life out of a useful function by the imposition of an irrelevant goal.

Another unlucky effect of the system is the swamping quantity of its products, the exposure of people to an endless stimulus of dramas, gags, panels, comment. Because of the frustrating content and form, none of these can speak profoundly or finish, so there is continual stimulation and inadequate discharge, and there-

fore compulsion to repeat. As with much of the rest of
the American standard of living, the system flourishes
by *preventing* serious or absorbing satisfaction.

Book publishing is essentially exempt from the specific interlocking system that we have been describing,
though it has important connections with it, *e.g.* the
concocting of non-books by the magazines, pre-
publication serialization, post-publication abstracting.
By and large, it is at present through books rather than
newspapers, magazines, or broadcasting that there is a
dissemination of non-standard information, editorial
dissent, muckraking, political and social analysis, exploration of sensibility. The fact that dissenting or ana-
lytic books sometimes sell a million copies, and must
have several million readers, proves that there is *not* a
lack of audiences with genuine interests.

But the book business has its own overcentralization
that results in concocting products by formula. (These
are not books, for a book is made by going through the
literary process.) The publishers' overhead, the capitalization of huge presses, the perquisites of the print-
ers' union require guaranteed sales to set so much capital in motion, and therefore reliance on big sales
forces, pre-planned promotion, and even marketing research for "ideas." I have been frequently chastened, as
an author, to find that the annual meeting of the salesmen is the only consideration for publication date, and
certainly not any wish of mine to reach a public on a
live issue. To turn over their investment quickly, also,
publishers make stabs at quick killings, publishing too
big editions of books on ephemeral subjects, and at
once remaindering the stock. And more and more of
the business has nothing to do with books at all, but is a
calculation of tie-ins with the movies, book clubs, serial
rights, reprint rights.

Finally, throughout communications, as in education, the method of organization is almost fatal in its mechanism of selecting its top-managers, responsible for policy and final decision of cases. The men who get to the top are not men who should wield cultural power. The means by which men rise in mass communications (and education) are not such as are most relevant to the advancement of the arts or inspiriting the body politic. There are exceptions in publishing, but I have not heard of any in big journalism or big broadcasting.

5

As the last of these assorted examples of overcentralization, let us consider the present organization of food production and distribution. This system is peculiarly anomalous because although, like the car complex, it has profoundly and unwittingly deranged the community, it is not even efficient for its internal purpose of maximizing profits, not to speak of producing goods. In principle—by Borsodi's Law—while high capitalization and standardization may reduce the unit-cost of production and packaging, nevertheless, with bulky and perishable commodities like foodstuffs, the unit-cost of distribution—transportation and retailing —must necessarily rise appreciably and perhaps eat up the prior savings. This was the experience of the Soviet state farms (although in that case there were many other unfavorable factors); but it seems to be the case also with our much more skilled farm and chain-grocery complexes.

At present in the United States, 70 per cent of all money spent on food goes to corporate and "cooperative" chains (not, of course, Rochdale cooperatives, which are democratically controlled and decentralized). Fifty per cent goes to fewer than a hundred of these; almost 30 per cent to the ten largest. In this system, both the retailers and the farmers have fallen under the control of the chains. The farmers contract beforehand to provide produce at the right time, to grow what can be transported long distances and what is most convenient for canning and freezing on a mass scale and for mass sales. Chains increasingly do the processing under their own brand names; and they intervene even more directly in food production by buying up and fattening livestock in their own corrals and so controlling the price.

Yet what is the result of this apparent rationalization, considered merely economically? Persistently the farmer's share of the take has dwindled, *e.g.* from 44 per cent in 1953 to 38 per cent in 1963. Prices to the consumer have not fallen or have even tended to rise. Nevertheless, the supermarkets claim, their profits on retail sales are only one per cent and there is lively competition among the chains and every effort to undercut and give bargains. And the chains have fought bitterly against the application of minimum-wage laws to their clerks, on the grounds that they cannot afford to pay a minimum wage.

If these claims of the chains are candid, the only explanation is that more and more of the take has dribbled away in the middle, in processing, packaging, transport, and jobbing. This money indeed does go to the big combinations, but it is entirely irrelevant to the primary function of growing food and feeding a population. It is a remarkable confirmation of Borsodi's Law.

The rationalized system has, without doubt, increased the consumer's variety of choice, foods out of season, pre-cooked meals, and *Woman's Day*. It has rather diminished the supply of fresh food in season. Here again, as with the improvements of the cars, the advantages on balance are a matter of opinion. The hybrids chosen for processing, transportability, and appearance are often plenty tasteless. Some claim that grain-fattened beef is inferior to range-fed Australian beef, not to speak of the watering. There *is* no substitute for fresh local vegetables and fruit. And, as with TV, preserving and cooking to please every taste result in the bland and sensational that dull every taste. Certainly too many pesticides are used too carelessly. The self-service and check-out system was, in my opinion, a fine invention of the supermarkets—it has been imitated by independent grocers—but, as is common in our society that purportedly has so few jobs to employ its people, there is never enough help to check you out and give such service as is needed. The Retail Clerks complain of the speed-up: "In a chain store, when a man's past forty and can't run any more, they look for a young guy to ease him out." (Earl Mc-David.)

The food is like much, and more and more, of the American standard of living: showy and shoddy. We had a good idea that worked up to a point; pushed beyond that point, the quantity is destroying the quality.

In its effects on the community, the chain-grocer system is an unmitigated disaster. Packaging assumes fantastic importance and consumers are more and more ignorant. Typically, they will pay several cents more for a brand-name bleach although a local bottle is labeled as identical in every respect. The anonymity and anomie of urban neighborhoods deteriorate further because independent grocers are forced out, even though there is no technological reason for it. A characteristic urban pattern is that tenants and tradesmen are dislocated by bulldozing for urban renewal, and after reconstruction, a big chain store moves in. (Consider an important contrary pattern: a major cause for the rather rapid Puerto Rican assimilation in big cities, as contrasted with the longer-resident Ne-groes, is that their extended families and exotic needs support many tiny grocery stores and restaurants, which give employment and accumulate capital, and provide social centers.)

Worst of all, the overcentralization in the food busi-ness has spelled the end of farming-as-a-way-of-life be-yond what is technically necessary or economically expedient. The system requires large-scale single-cropping and forces out small operators. (With miser-able social planning, the government subsidies also fa-vor the big operators.) The long-term pre-contracting rules out the diversification, weather-wisdom, wind-falls, and multiple skills by which an intelligent man can gain advantages. In towns and cities, farmers' mar-kets for independent grocers have closed up. It is as-serted that people have spontaneously quit rural life because of the lure of the city; but there is evidence to the contrary—a small rise in the farmer's take for milk, for instance, results in marginal farms resuming opera-tion; but of course this process cannot often be re-peated. In any case, the present conditions that await them in the cities are such that farm youth should be discouraged by every means from leaving what they have. But the brute fact is that, under the terms set by the present system, small farmers cannot make a go of it.

Truck gardens have vanished from the vicinity of big cities to be replaced by urban sprawl in the form of suburban developments, whereas the farms could have been an elegant and immensely functional part of green-belt and satellite planning. Other regions, *e.g.* northern New England or northern Wisconsin, have become depopulated and had their rail service discon-tinued, but they will no doubt eventually be redevel-oped as resorts and recreation areas. This process can be somberly compared to the eighteenth-century enclosures, and there are plenty of Deserted Villages. Our barons do this kind of thing in our own style.

As we have seen, the chain stores complain of the intense competition that keeps down their rate of profit. Their system has not matured to the point of semi-monopoly and fixed prices—though there is price fixing in beef. Once the independents are quite out of the picture, however, it will be possible to set prices at whatever level the centralized system calls for, no matter how inefficient it may be in some ideal sense. There will then in fact be no group skilled enough to compete. The careful demonstrations of Borsodi that even family subsistence farming, with small electrical machines, is often more efficient (in hours and minutes of labor) than big operation, will then seem patently absurd. Nobody will be able to imagine such a thing. In brief, as for many other areas, the inevitability of centralism will be self-proving. A system destroys its competitors by pre-empting the means and channels, and then proves that it is the only conceivable mode of operating.

In both this country and other parts of the world, we are in a period of excessive urbanization, that makes no sense as regional planning or as community planning. In this process, excessive centralization has usually been a major contributory cause, by making the more organic life of the country unviable, and by offering immensely inflated wages which then vanish in urban poverty. People who were poor and had food now cannot subsist on ten or fifty times the income. Certainly a major goal of empirical decentralism is to find kinds of rural-urban symbiosis to support rural rehabilitation, perhaps to increase the rural ratio in the United States from 8 per cent to something like 20 per cent. And in this effort, perhaps even a revival of small cash-cropping is *not* out of the question.

Consider it this way: It is now the settled policy of our government to get seven million more farm folk off the land, since they are economically a drag. These farmers will then go to a city where the cheapest kind of public housing costs $18,000 a unit; that is, one could subsidize the farmer $1,000 a year for eighteen years to stay in his own farmhouse rather than to leave—not counting his likelihood of ending up on relief, whereas on the farm he largely fed himself and his family. But of course this is the same society that, on grounds of economic efficiency, has made supernumeraries of twenty million Negroes, of everybody over sixty-five years of age, and of the majority of the young who are kept in schools that are useless to them, simply to keep them off the streets. Is this really the most *economical* way of running things?

yes!

6

In these four examples we see how an enterprise loses touch with its function or utility by imposing the abstract goal of the organization and becoming increasingly irrelevant. In the schools by the aggrandizement of the bureaucracy. In the cars and roads by the hypertrophy of the product. In communications by standardization; as Norbert Wiener pointed out, repeating the same message increases the noise of a communications system and prevents information. In the food business by pushing a method essentially self-defeating.

Perhaps more significant is that the very aggrandizement of the organization, without countervailing forces, leads to far-reaching destructive social effects that were not at all intended.

In three of these examples, however, the abstract goal of the organization is really making money, and it might be claimed that this is the cause of the ill effects and the loss of function. This is the claim of socialists, who say that without wasteful competition and with still more planning, everything would be splendid. But if we turn to a centralizing socialism like the Russian, we find that in two of the functions, communications and farms, even without the profit motive, the method of organization has led to even worse regimentation, disruption, dullness, and inefficiency, because of other abstract goals, ideology, and *raison d'état*. With regard to the schools, there is no direct question of profit in the United States or in Russia (I assume that peculation is universal), but although I would match our bureaucracy against the world, the Russians *are* famous in this line. With regard to the cars, however, the Russians have been making more sensible and discriminating choices than we.

Overcentralization is an international disease of modern times. It transcends political ideologies. It is endemic in the warring power structure and in the misuse of modern technology. It will show up in darkest Africa as the new States make their great leaps "forward."

In my opinion, the profit motive as such can be more or less benign, depending on the context. Cases must be decided on their merits. Suppose we set as our modest goal the maximum of social safety (including a moderate freedom from being pushed around) plus some liveliness in order that life can go on. Then, to revert to our present examples: In the case of communications, if the broadcasting channels can be considerably decentralized—*e.g.* by giving over the TV ultra-high-frequency channels to profit and non-profit independents—commercial competitiveness might make a perfectly viable situation. In the case of the cars, however, with their absolute determining of patterns of community, I can see no alternative but to treat the whole complex as a natural monopoly and to regulate it. The profit motive has here proved too virulent.

7

Except for Populism, the major party conflicts of the past century have *not* been about our subject, whether we think of Whig, Democrat, Tory, Nationalist, Labor, Radical, Socialist, or Fascist. Class struggle, sectional struggle, struggle of interest groups have been for control of the growing centralized power rather than limitation or division of it. In campaign speeches, of course, there has been no lack of complaints about "bigness," "big Business," "big Government," expressed by the party on the out; but these ideas have been rhetorical and have almost never led to attempts to carry them through. Thus, both the empty rhetoric and the absence of concrete remedies have created the impression that the growing centralization is historically inevitable, because of technical advance, increase of population, or increase of wealth. And nowadays, a philosopher like Jacques Ellul holds that the progress of technique and the dehumanizing effects of overcentralization are identical and entirely beyond human control; he finally finds no distinction between "technology" and the method of political and social organization; in our times, there *is* no alternative way of life. But I think he is himself suffering from the brainwashing that he accurately describes. In my opinion, the sense of historical inevitability is the *result* of the lack of political attention and not the cause of it. There would now be more decentralization (with perhaps a *more* advanced technology!) if there had been a political struggle for it, as there was in the eighteenth century.

(To put it crudely: more than any other factor, it is the increasing size and destructiveness of the wars that have saddled us with our present excessive centralization. This subject is beyond the scope of this book, but I try to spell it out in Appendix I.)

Conversely, during the same period, the moral and social philosophers who have been critical of centralization, human rationalization, and collectivism, have wildly varied in their political and economic tendencies. Coleridge was an Establishment conservative, Madison a democrat, Bakunin almost a permanent-revolutionist, and Sorel almost a fascist. Proudhon maintained private property, Kropotkin was a communist. William Morris wanted to cut back on technology, Patrick Geddes thought that big new technology would bring decentralist liberty, and Borsodi and Aldous Huxley relied on small new technology. Wright was paternalistic, Mumford is rather administrative, Biddle a community-developer, and Malatesta was a libertarian. In a striking way, *all* of these philosophers have been out of the mainstream of nineteenth- and twentieth-century "politics," which have been capitalist, statist, welfare-statist, nationalist, or Marxist. In an equally striking way (it seems to me), all of them speak to the political unease of our own times.

CHAPTER IV

Un-free Enterprise

1

The centralizing social style we have been describing is very productive, not only in the quantity and variety of goods but also in producing new things and ways and transforming the landscape. As I have pointed out elsewhere, no "utopian" planner, following a dogmatic blueprint, would ever dare, or want, to institute such radical and rapid changes in the social pattern and in the geography of the country as the cars, TV, air travel, computers, the drive to higher education, have brought about in a generation or less. This is the forcefulness and ferment of America that appeals to visitors from more stolid regions like Australia.

It is also the case, however, that these continual revolutionary alterations are wild and increasingly irrelevant to what anyone would choose; their effects on individuals are, by and large, harrying rather than stimulating, drastic but superficial. The products and effects pour as if from systems running for their own sake. But this is not, in my opinion, because there is not enough planning. There is an enormous amount of planning at every level and with regard to every kind of function from hardware to high culture and mental disease. It is that the planners, managers, and producers are not free and choosing human beings in relation to what they are doing. To achieve communal, artistic, and scientific products, humanity must be built into an enterprise at every step; but in our enterprises, human choice is ceasing to operate at any step. Trapped in a system, people carry on functions often fraught with colossal or catastrophic consequences without being personally engaged in the functions at all. They are personnel.

In the following chapters let us explore the relations, in this style, between producers and their products. What happens to enterprise? What happens to function and cost? What happens to moral engagement?

2

Assume, for the sake of analysis, that the top-direction of a very large centralized corporation is very wise and devoted to the goal of the organization. Nevertheless, being one man or a small group, top-management does not have enough *mind* to do an adequate job. There are simply not enough points of view and there is not enough energy or attention to cope with the multifarious social and technical details that arise. And in fact, the evidence is that top-managers—and independent professionals—are the most overworked members of society. They are likely to put in sixty to ninety hours a week. They cannot be protected by a schedule because they are responsible; they *must* meet the situations. To deputize authority does not help, because one then exhausts more time in briefings and committee meetings than if one tried to control everything one-self. In the end, the overwork is stupefying.

Top-management cannot be departmentalized. A manager cannot restrict himself to policy, but must be the final judge of application to doubtful and new cases as well. If because of pressure of time unique cases are treated as routine, a manager's expert judgment is useless. We saw this in the case of the report on Panama that was filed and forgotten.

Meantime, as the head, the manager represents his organization in its extramural relations also, as spokesman or defendant or in answering correspondence. Eighty per cent of the working time of college presidents, for instance, according to John Corson's manual on college administration, is wasted with alumni, athletic coaches, public speeches, and cases of discipline. Needless to say, in such extramural relations, a manager must resort to clichés and to lack of candor, and this is stupefying to himself as well as to others.

3

There are intrinsic difficulties in information and feedback. Being at a desk in headquarters, a manager must depend on the information that is communicated upward from the field. Assume that his informants are earnest and honest. Nevertheless, at each level of transmission upward the information must be abstracted and processed in order to be usable by the superior. Every such product is an approximation, and some properties are left out altogether. With the accumulation of mere approximations and omissions, the information received by the manager is often useless or false. Thus he becomes objectively stupider about his business. (By contrast, Haroun Al Raschid used to disguise himself as a commoner and go into the street to find out what was going on; but during this time of day, of course, he was not at his desk in headquarters.)

A field worker, in direct contact with the material, may hit on an invention, and in scientific management there is provided a suggestion box for ideas to be communicated upward to the chief. But the foreman, who was not hired to judge good ideas but to discipline men, thinks that the idea is not worth passing on and wasting the superiors' time, so he files it. Or again, one tries to get a report from a government agency, but it is refused as secret. One phones the chief of the bureau and is at once sent the report, because it is not secret. But in this case, the subordinate too knows that it is not secret. However, if he happened to clear a document and something went wrong, he would be to blame; so it is safer to refuse as many requests as possible.

Or proceed from the top down. A policy is decided, and to make sure that it is understood and correctly executed, it is simplified and a procedure is standardized. In a large organization, such standardization is essential, e.g. the profile acceptable in hiring. But of course the standard misfits every actual instance. Peculiar appropriateness is ruled out like any other peculiarity. It is almost impossible for the best procedure to be used except clandestinely, or for the best man to be employed unless he goes through unusual channels. The wise manager understands that this is the score, but he is hamstrung by his own directive. For instance, it is even characteristic of big organizations to drop a first-rate man because of public relations or some other abstraction. A manager has to learn to harden his heart and stupefy his good sense.

Consider now an extreme, but not unique, case when the logistics of sheer size get out of hand. I am quoting from an interview of Daniel Lang with Walter Skallerup of the nuclear Human Reliability Program.

The Reliability Program covers all men who have "the knowledge and opportunity" to make trouble at nuclear stations. "Emotional checks" have been run on a quarter of a million men in the Air Force alone. Of that number, thousands were judged to need clinical evaluation, and of those a significant number were transferred from nuclear duty. . . . "It's a delicate balance that we're trying to strike," Skallerup said. "We want the men stable but not phlegmatic. We don't want to hurt their spirit, yet we have to keep them toeing the line."

Is it the fact that there are questionnaires, variables, profiles, and computation adequate to this kind of problem? I don't mean that I know any other way of organizing this *particular* enterprise, for insane premises necessarily produce absurd dilemmas.

4

Subordinates tend to become stupider more rapidly and directly, simply because they cannot learn anything by exercising initiative and taking responsibility. Stultification occurs acutely when a man is bright and sees a better way to do something, but must follow a worse directive; this is a grim experience and cannot be thrice repeated without going numb. Every top-down system is grounded in the assumption that each man is competent in the task assigned to him but that he has no notions about anything else or about the whole operation. But in fact every man has all kinds of notions, some vague or foolish, some clear and critical. By the time that a man is indeed thinking only about his own detail, he has become a stupid ox indeed. Most of his mental energy is likely to be bound up in willed inattention.

Another kind of subordinate is the spirited man with a departmentalized function that employs only a fraction of his energy and ability, but who therefore builds it up into an elaborate drama or kingdom of his own that can more totally engage his interest and emotions. A vast proportion of bureaucratic pedantry and intra-mural politicking certainly has this origin. It is intensely subtle, and sharp, and stupid. A pathetic example is the rewrite man on a national magazine who spends days and nights at the almost impossible task of rewriting the clear and close prose of good authors; but he must have something to occupy himself with and earn his keep.

When a man or department is successfully departmentalized, however, it becomes a point of correctness and pride to refuse to consider anything that does not exactly fit one's competence. Unfortunately, departments dovetail only in the abstract plan; or sometimes they do not dovetail at all, if the original plan was poor or conditions have changed. Thus, some items may fail to win any attention at all and be neglected. This hang-up is very trying in the case of multifunctional projects in government. If a project, *e.g.* a good youth work camp, involves labor *and* education *and* conservation, it may happen that no department will sponsor it. (This contrasts curiously with the brilliant use that industrial corporations make of their by-products.) And as we pointed out in *Communitas*, though a great city has dozens of agencies that bear on a particular community problem, there is no way to handle the interrelation of aspects that is often the essence of a community problem.

The preferred method of finally coping with gaps of jurisdiction is to add still another agency. It is not to alter the faulty organizational plan. For instance, in the rapid development of science, important teaching often falls outside or across the old university departments—biophysics, mathematical sociology, ecology.

Yet the old departments will not relinquish their required courses; rather, the student must bear a double load. So organizations get bigger by mere inertia.

The more reasonable way of improving communication, to increase people's awareness and concern, so that they can and will cope with organic relations, is against the spirit of centralization, the subdivision of function. It is not easy to give a rating for organic awareness. There is, however, a new department of Generalism; a generalist is a man expert in higher-level abstractions, for instance the perfect University President. Such people tend to know nothing at all.

5

Managers, we have seen, work hard and long. The job is their show and they must think it worthwhile and useful. Subordinates, however, are restricted in both initiative and self-expression and their motivation is likely to be merely extrinsic, rise in status and salary.

Extrinsic motivation confuses the doing of a task even further, for role playing and the appearance of performance are as good as the real thing. And a man will go over to a rival firm or quit the business altogether if he gets a better deal. Conversely, management feels no loyalty to the subordinates, for the group is bound together not by a common enterprise but only by extrinsic rewards.

All this is taken for granted and perhaps makes little difference when the main purpose of the enterprise is itself extrinsic, to make money. (Incidentally, the meaning of "entrepreneur" has gotten to be not a man who mounts an enterprise but a man out to make money. I think this would have sickened Adam Smith.) Given such a purpose, the consortium of manager and subordinates all on the make might even result in a sharp team. But if the purpose of the organization is to provide useful goods and services, the cross purposes of management and subordinates, the one wanting to do a job and the others wanting to get a raise, can be a serious obstacle. Or it can work the other way: *e.g.* a professor may want to teach and do serious scholarship, but the management wants publications in order to upgrade the institution.

A subordinate who is not ambitious to rise—perhaps he is resigned or has outside interests—may become a time-server. If this becomes the general tone, the organization bogs down into a routine and begins to run for its own sake. Such a development is terribly frustrating to an energetic manager; yet he, too, after firing a few of the time-servers, must resign himself to lower his sights. It is at this point that the concept of "Security" begins to loom large, for both the subordinates and the manager. Without a pretty strong will to try hard, any departure from the routine looks risky; and, on the other hand, a big organization that has plenty of accustomed clients or customers can go a long way on its own momentum, so long as the surrounding conditions do not become suddenly unfavorable and so long as nobody inquires too nicely. It is felt, truly or falsely, that where so much capital and so many vested interests are at stake, it is best to be "conservative." Novelty or experiment involves dislocations that are not worth the trouble.

At this point, management too will go in for face-saving *apologiae* like any bureaucratic subordinate. And this is not necessarily a bad symbiosis. There might be far more loyalty and *esprit de corps* in a time-serving organization, though of course little morale.

Running for its own sake, an organization can quite lose touch with its ostensible function and with the environment. Its real function is now to protect, reward,

incestuously recruit its personnel. There is no telling
the results. Its chief business might become paper
work, public relations, and the maintenance of routine
production. Or, alternatively, especially if there are no
countervailing forces, and if the climate nourishes expansion, the enterprise may run wild, like rabbits or
poison ivy. It may enter every field, do them all badly,
and make tons of money.

6

Return now to our very wise manager. When big
systems run on their own, new management will be
chosen for systematic rather than functional reasons.
There are various possibilities. Those who rise to the
top may be safe men, who upset no apple carts. They
will be those who get along by understanding and sharing the extrinsic motives of everybody else; or perhaps
they exercise duplicity in that direction until they
have acquired power and can be ruthless. They usually
will have been reliable supporters of existing management and so have won promotion over the other jun-
iors. Yet the exact opposite also occurs: an outsider
who has made a great name in some other firm is imported, to get things moving, to branch out in a new
line. It is not remembered that he may have risen in the
other firm by the same non-functional arts, and it is
often astounding what tiny accomplishments are
thought to prove excellence—they might consist of
having been mentioned in *Time*. Or a less conspicuous
stranger, a dark horse, may be imported simply because neither of two powerful factions in an organization will give the other the satisfaction.

In my opinion, the salient cause of ineptitude in promotion and in all hiring practices is that, under centralized conditions, fewer and fewer know what *is* a good
job of work. The appearance of competence may

count for more than the reality, and it is a lifework to manufacture appearance or, more usually, to adapt to the common expectation. Just as there is reliance on extrinsic motives, there is heavy reliance on extrinsic earmarks of competence: testing, profiles, publications, hearsay among wives, flashy *curricula vitae*. Yet there is no alternative method of selection. In decentralized conditions, where a man knows what goes on and engages in the whole enterprise, an applicant can present a masterpiece for examination and he has functional peers who can decide whether they want him in the guild. To be sure, he might then be rejected because he is too competent rather than not competent enough. (There is no possible method of social organization to make the outstanding acceptable.) But at least he can try elsewhere and get another real hearing.

There is no test for performing a highly departmentalized role except evidence of playing a role and of ability at routine skills. Inevitably, the negative criteria for selection become preponderant—the reasons why a man won't do—and so the whole enterprise becomes still stupider. To give an analogy that is also an example: when a prize art work is selected by a mixed jury, each member of the jury has to renounce what in his heart he knows *is* art, and the selection will be something innocuous that is competent or looks like art. (On the other hand—and this is an analogy to decentralism—if the jury is packed, the selection will confirm the common prejudice of the jurors but not be strong enough to arouse envy; it will, however, have to be genuine.)

In brief, as those who judge—colleagues, consumers, the electorate—become stupid, management also becomes stupid. So after a while we cannot maintain the assumption that in established firms top-management *can* be wise and capable.

To be candid, I would take this analysis for a mere satire with elements of truth, except that, candidly, I cannot otherwise explain to myself how the people I meet, both directors and subordinates, who are obviously intelligent, honest, well intentioned, and fairly imaginative, nevertheless work so incredibly dully and stupidly, and produce products that are routine or disastrous, in manufacture, government, journalism, or education. So far below human capability. My conclusion is that it must be the conditions of the work itself.

7

But in proportion as such systems render their own people powerless, outside their ostensible function they exert crushing power, often unwittingly. For activity cannot make social sense without mind and concern at every step. And the more they blunder, the more they step on other people's toes. Besides, large systems pre-empt the social means and space for carrying on the function at all. There is no way to be effective outside the system, and within the system the function is debased. This is, of course, the commonplace that keeps the "best" people out of politics.

It is possible for small enterprises, requiring special skills and producing a highly tailored product, to survive, but it is really not easy to think of major examples. I mentioned the Puerto Rican grocers; free-lance writers and artists are an important group; and there must be a few others. But we have seen that neighborhood grocers, mechanics and repair men, and small farmers are forced into the big systems, though such enterprises require small capital and would seem to invite independents. The crucial class of researchers and inventors is bought up. And even autonomous and highly unique enterprises, like colleges, dance groups, or art galleries, are profoundly deranged by centraliz-

ing processes sometimes meant only to help and subsidize them. Recently, for instance, there has been a justified outcry that a large foundation grant to one school
of ballet has dealt a death-blow to more lively schools
of ballet. Where large capital is involved, *e.g.* for architecture or to promote inventions, escape is impossible.

Excuse me if I report a very tiny example to illustrate the difficulties of enterprise. "A modest volunteer
group of youngsters had made themselves into a kind
of domestic peace corps and had fixed up the interior
courtyard of a slum block in Harlem. Their access to
the interior had been by means of a City-owned lot,
approximately 100 by 25 feet. . . . However, last
week, the Commissioner of Real Estate, in his zeal to
pick up a few pennies for the City, sold the property
for $600. The purchaser immediately turned around
and offered to sell it back to the civil rights group—
the Harlem Education Project—for $4,000." (Mary
Perot Nichols in *The Village Voice.*) These youngsters do not have $4,000.

There is no telling how many people with inventive
ideas and plenty of initiative, but who have to do
things their own way, become discouraged and give
up. This type, either as epic or tragic hero, no longer
appears in literature except, significantly, in the frantic
bathos of the Radical Right, as in Ayn Rand. The
more common story is for talent to be bought up and
to become resigned. *E.g.* I once sent the *New Yorker* a
story, which happened to be factual, about an architect
who refused a commission because it involved tearing
down a fine building by an illustrious predecessor; I
was told that the consensus of the editors was that no
professional would act that way. What is most discouraging to an inventive man, perhaps, is to see his
good idea apparently accepted by big operators, and

then shelved, worked over, standardized and sanitized beyond recognition, or used for an opposite purpose than he intended. It would be interesting to study the fate of the bright youngsters who went to Washington with Kennedy. Many have quit. (Some of these have not quit the *field*, but have set up as independent consultants across the street, hoping to have more effect in the long run by working outside the system.)

Here is an example of discouragement by government: When the government began seriously to underwrite scientific research, excellent scientists accepted the arduous duty of reviewing proposals, and they selected a small number as both promising and needing this particular kind of support. But it happened that so much money had been budgeted that support was given to a great number of projects, many of them factitious. The time of the scientists had been wasted. Any bureaucrats could have done as well.

Here is a similar case from private enterprise: In a big publishing house, an editor was responsible to select twenty books a year to keep the overhead in action. In fact, only about six worthy manuscripts crossed his desk, so he handed in his list of twenty with the six starred as the authentic books. Yet only two of the starred items, but most of the others, were accepted by management. The editor quit.

And here is a modest and terribly common kind of case occurring forever in both public and private enterprises: A fellow looks for a simple job as laborer or stock clerk, and he finds that he must fill out forms and answer questions that are entirely irrelevant to the task, but that he cannot safely answer; or perhaps he is terrorized by forms altogether or can't read. He quits looking.

Let me say, however, that decentralized and voluntary organizations also make life tough by irrelevant moral, religious, or racial requirements. In fact it is a specialty of the house. As I pointed out in discussing the New York school system, it is a human advantage of established bureaucracies and management-union combinations that they have due-process and grievance committees, to avoid arbitrary injustice. But the worst possible arrangements are those that combine the irrelevancies of both centralization and decentralization. On the one hand, a big corporation that demands petty moral conformity as if it were a small-town gossip group. On the other hand, a tiny voluntary peace organization that sets standards of dress for the sake of public relations, as if it were J. P. Morgan's bank.

8

When the social means are tied up in such complicated organizations, it becomes extraordinarily difficult and sometimes impossible to do a simple thing directly, even though the doing is common sense and would meet with universal approval, as when neither the child, nor the parent, nor the janitor, nor the principal of the school can remove the offending door catch. There is created a mandarinism, in which too many things are done according to protocol. Eagerness, appetite, inspiration, common sense are stymied by licenses, merely formal standards, due process, the need to confront stuffed shirts, and, as we shall see in the next chapter, the need for amounts of capital out of all proportion to the nature of the enterprise. This last point deserves special emphasis. It is not kept in mind, by either conservatives or liberals, that mandarinism is most disadvantageous to poor people. The corporations that complain about red tape also have accountants and lawyers.

Innocently and unwittingly—isn't it ironical how many of the effects of logistics and rationalization are unwitting?—the climate of "efficiency" is brutally repressive of poor and simple people, even when the deliberate purpose is to assist them and break down class barriers. The middle class is less hurt because it has internalized the obsessional, abstract and indirect, style; linguistic studies have shown how this style is already transmitted at age three and four (Basil Bernstein). But poor people who cannot cope in this "formal" style become still poorer. Schools, social agencies, clinics rush to help them with massive doses of the same formal procedure.

The aim of liberals is certainly not to make the poor dependent but to give them opportunity so that they can become self-reliant. The effect of liberal procedure is to stupefy the poor still further, by long hours of waiting on lines and taking aptitude and achievement tests. Yet professionals have a superstitious belief in their methods.

It is a mass-superstition, pervasive and irresistible. I have before me as an examiner a senior thesis in which the student proves by means of two batteries of projective tests administered in several high schools that—frustration tends to get people angry. Rather tartly, I point out to him that this is what his complicated phraseology boils down to, and I ask him to suggest twenty-five experiments on man and beast that could more directly confirm this newsy hypothesis. With a small show of resentment, he dutifully complies, but so far as I can see, he doesn't get the point. I am at a loss how to grade him. But if I fail to grade him, how will he make State U. for his M.A. in sociology? Their machine would not even eat his application, and I would become engaged in Correspondence. Terrorized by this last thought, I give him an *A*.

A Negro graduate student of mine has a plan to tutor middle-adolescent Negroes in his neighborhood

who are failing in school. He corrals some other graduate students, gets the use of the basement of his
church as a "facility," and asks the school system (Mil-
waukee) for the names of the kids to contact. But no;
this kind of thing is now cleared through the Urban
League. My student goes to the Urban League. No; the
idea is a good one, but the Urban League and the
school system have a joint program with a great Catholic university that provides the personnel to implement
such ideas. The Catholic university duly sends some
sweet girls from a suburban finishing school, and they
are terrified by the hulking sixteen- and seventeen-year-
olds and do not reappear. . . . But my student is persistent. He gets the names under the table from a couple of guidance counselors in the high schools, and he
proceeds unofficially.

Suppose you have a similar concrete task that wants
doing and you need a grant-in-aid. As I have pointed
out, it is better to call it a Pilot Project, cook it up in
these terms, and ask for ten times as much money, for
by the new metaphysics a one-shot or small-scale enterprise is nothing at all. You protest that you do not
mean to be doing scientific research but just to make
your street more livable. Ah, in that case, you can
probably get an Intern from Urban Renewal or Home
Finance, as a Project Assistant. What! you don't *need*
an assistant?

Many talented persons do not know the arts, move
in the right circles, or have the disposition to cope in
the present organization of enterprise; and rather
likely, many who do know the ropes are pretty cynical
performers or have no other abilities at all. Of course it
is not a new thing that virtue and talent are misfits
while phonies flourish. The literary "scene" in *Les Il-
lusions Perdues* is very like the literary "scene" forever, and *An Enemy of the People* was not written in

America and not last week. But we have added something new, the general agreement that unorganized excellence does not exist, has no right to exist, and if she exists we know how to make an honest woman of her.

The Americans suffer from an ambivalence. On the one hand, as the feeling of powerlessness spreads, there is a deep conviction that "Nothing Can Be Done" because of the machinery that has to be set in motion, even when the problem or the abuse is simple and something can easily be done. On the other hand, identifying with the big symbols and institutions, people have a conviction that they are powerful, that they have "mastered" Nature, that technology, administration, and plain bullying are omnicompetent. Each term of the ambivalence lends emotional energy and confirming behavior to the other. The more powerless people are, the more they put their faith in princes; and the more they put their faith in princes, the more powerless they are.

9

If we review historically the components of the present centralizing style, we can remember what immense advantages they entailed in their time and circumstances. The cash-accounting of the commercial revolution. The political centralism of the rise of the national states. The method of bureaucratic administration developed during the eighteenth century. The standardization and rationalization of product and process brought in by the Industrial Revolution. The interlocking of the whole by political economy. Most recently, the systematic development of scientific technology.

Yet, unfortunately, in combination these components have progressively and cumulatively created a bind that closes out new thought, relevance, and freedom of choice, and that invades every detail of life.

We too have our time and circumstances. As I have said, centralism is a poor frame of mind with which to confront unprecedented problems of automation, urbanization, mass communications, nuclear weapons, the breakdown of colonialism, the organization of one world. These circumstances, novel and dangerous, are confusing at best. When they are confronted by compulsively repeating an invariable pattern of thought, they become intractable.

Put it this way: If we practiced medicine according to the Renaissance, baroque, rococo, and robber-baron conceptions that seem to do for our politics, business, and technology, we should certainly all be dead of the bubonic plague. It is appalling to witness the rise of the nation-states in Africa, the methods by which grown men parley on how not to blow the world to bits, the petty cash-accounting used in the education of the young and in rebuilding cities, the process by which we choose leaders and invest them with power, the berserk multiplication of things that clutter up time and space. For each of these, any bright child could think up more effective or prudent behavior. I don't mean to say, however, that I know of any brilliant solutions by anybody for the essential thing, how to make it all work together.

But the bother is that we continually take for granted a basic bad idea and then exhaust mind and energy in tinkering and patching. At a political convention, the prudent try frantically to prevent gross mistakes, but the party machinery was inept long before. Scientists try desperately to get a test ban because of the fallout, but their whole relation to power has been erroneous long before. Educators are at a loss as to how to cope with an enrollment that makes scholarship impossible, but they themselves have encouraged the superstition of schooling. Great powers go to the brink of suicide to neutralize one another's dangerous influence in small countries, but all their practice is to exploit, corrupt, and tempt the small countries, for that is what it means to be a great power.

And characteristically, the archaic behavior is served by such beautiful modern technology that it itself seems to make sense or to be at least plausible. At the political convention, delegates act like baboons from every angle on the TV. Traffic congestion is timed by an electronic computer. Between the President and the Premier there can be instant communication across seven thousand miles. Thus, everything possible is being taken care of, isn't it? By the best means that the human intellect can devise.

CHAPTER V

Comparative Costs

1

An objective way of measuring the degree of personal engagement of workmen in an enterprise, or of their intrinsic or extrinsic motivation for it, is to compare the costs of enterprises performing the "same" function with different methods of social organization. Plausibly, the less you have to pay a man to do a job, the more he is doing it because he wants to; and the less spent on administration and overhead, the more directly people are engaged in what they are doing. Of course, most of the time there are crucial other factors that prevent free contract—*e.g.* dishwashers doing the most onerous work get a dollar an hour if they are lucky, and Puerto Ricans working for charity hospitals or Columbia University are not paid the usual minimum wages; but I think the rules apply in what follows. In this chapter, I will analyze the comparative costs of half a dozen functions performed in centralized complexes and decentrally. These are mainly service enter-

prises with which I have had some personal acquaintance, and in these cases the decentral savings come to
three, five, and ten times. It pays to operate on a small
scale. In this range of functions, naturally, persons and administration are the major costs.

In another range of enterprises, *e.g.* mining or transportation (excluding taxis), small-scale operation is
now impossible or prohibitively expensive, and the savings from big capital outweigh the costs of personnel
and administration.* The same holds for much manufacturing. But my guess is that in the manufacture of
many kinds of big hardware, the least costly arrangement is a mixture of decentral operations within a
centralized operation, *e.g.* cottage manufacture, with
electrical tools, of parts collected and automatically as-
sembled; there would be big savings in commutation and
schedule. Home manufacture of machined parts was ob-
ligatory in England during the last war because of the
bombings, and it succeeded. Much of farming, on the
other hand, might prove to be most efficient if decentral within a decentral framework: farmers' voluntary
cooperatives for processing and regional marketing.
The farmers would get the middleman profits which
now go to the chains, and on the whole it would probably be a cheaper and certainly a simpler operation.

But it is stupid to have to speculate on questions that
are empirical. Where is the empirical information?
Certainly, compared to much of what is researched
these days, *this* subject is worth researching. At pres-

* But in other conditions, *cf.* (Reuters): "The Northern Rho-
desian government intends to promote the development of
small-scale mining in the rural areas to reduce the country's
dependence on its major industry—copper. 'We think it is
preferable to take mining to the people instead of letting the
people drift into the copper belt,' Prime Minister Kaunda explained. Elsewhere the economy is largely subsistence agriculture. Kaunda said small local mines could be worked by people
in conjunction with their agricultural activities.

ent, the moral and political advantages are entirely on the side of decentralizing where possible; and the economic savings, by cutting down administration, middlemen, and unproductive commutation, might well run into many billions of dollars.

2

Nevertheless, it is often, perhaps usually, impossible to make an accurate comparison of costs between different methods of operation, for the style of production powerfully effects the products themselves, the products are not exactly comparable, and it becomes a matter of opinion what different things are worth.

Differences of judgment are reflected in the market price; and with regard to centralized or decentralist style, market judgments of fashion or taste are quite weird. For instance, the products of skilled individual or local craftsmanship are sometimes highly prized, either because they are roughly finished, or because they are finely finished, or because they are tailor-made to order. Jobbers buy up peasant wares, and rich people make dressmakers and decorators rich. Yet at a higher level of performance, *e.g.* in entertainment, music, or education, the very same virtues are usually strongly disesteemed in comparison with the slick, standardized, or licensed style, including the standard folksy, which is alone considered to be professional, though it is entirely the artifact of central market processes. For the mass, as for children, the homemade is no good, and the authentic is regarded as amateurish. Underprivileged urban children in the country will not eat the fresh vegetables; if the food does not come from cans, they do not trust it not to be poison. Yet again, in the very same fields of entertainment and education, the homemade might suddenly be transformed into Fine

Art or Wisdom, and fetch either nothing or a fortune.
I myself am paid anywhere between $.oo and $1,000
for the same lecture.

Economists would not deny these vagaries of consumers, but they would say they are trivial compared
with the grand economic fact that, by and large, centralized organization of production and distribution
has beaten out independents and voluntary associations
in providing goods and services in a free market; therefore it must, by and large, cost less. And by and large
I agree—up to a point in history. Whatever the disval-
ues of the Industrial Revolution, its centralizing methods of concentrating capital, standardizing product and
process, regimenting labor, and organizing sales did
produce and distribute goods cheap. Yet the following
new factors must now be taken into account:

new costs

1. In later years there has been an increase of
hidden costs borne by the public, that are especially
advantageous to big systems but do not appear in
the price—*e.g.* the roads and cars, tax and mortgage policies that favor suburban and "project"
housing and disrupt neighborhoods and villages,
schools and colleges geared to state and corporate
needs, cheap postage and public TV channels carrying the ads.
2. By habituation and stultification over the years,
consumers are no longer able to judge worth. The
possibility of creating synthetic demand, the excessive installment buying, etc., are proof that
people no longer have alternative choices. Those
who speak of an Affluent Society do not mean a
society with a high-quality standard of living.
3. In important areas, there is no free market, but a
system of semi-monopolies with inflated overhead
expenses to avoid taxes, and fixed prices that do not

reflect reasonable costs. These combinations direct research, control patents, and parcel out improvements entirely to their own advantages.

4. Finally, the pre-emption of the social means and space and the destruction of initiative and skills have radically diminished competitive re-entry of independents according to classical economic laws. If we want them back, it must be as a result of social policy—and that is the reason for this book.

Under these conditions, it is not the case that an *all-pervasive* centralized style of production and distribution is evidently the most efficient. It is even improbable.

3

On Broadway, to rehearse and mount a modest play without music costs upward of $100,000; and $20,000 a week to run. The average for an off-Broadway production is $10,000 to $15,000 to mount, and $2,000 to $3,000 a week to run. We may assume that the two productions are professionally comparable; indeed, since 95 per cent of actors are always unemployed and always eager to appear, one is likely to see equivalent casts in either location. (Off-Broadway is usually not only livelier but more competent; but that is my opinion.)

The chief differential costs are salaries, nature of the staff, rent, payment for venture capital, and often a different rate of royalties. On Broadway, the minimum for Equity actors with bit parts is between $100 and $150 a week. The plays must be staffed by union stagehands, technicians, publicity men, and designers; and once a play is mounted, there is an almost comical amount of featherbedding. The formal Broadway theater, ushers, program, come to high rent. The legal fee for a specialist in theater law may come to $1,000 to draw the contracts.

Off-Broadway—in theaters with fewer than 299 seats—union actors can work for subsistence, say $40 a week. A stand-by may get $10 a week, just to have learned the role and to be on tap. Staffing is generally done by the company itself and is strictly functional —the various theater unions agree not to notice the transgressions. The theater is informal and is often a relatively cheap space (there is no really cheap space in New York City) remodeled by the company. The ushers are friends or members of the company. Legal advice comes from a judge who is a relative, or a law student at N. Y. U. Members of the company are likely to act, build sets, design, sit in the box office, and so forth.

Profits from a Broadway hit are large, but so are the risks. In average seasons, four out of five plays may flop, and most of these will be a total loss. The cost of capital is corresponding. And, inevitably, this situation powerfully influences the choice of plays and style of acting and production, toward star names, a glamorous or sophisticated professionalism never far from commonplace, plots that contain the expected with a twist. Actors polish themselves according to this standard, whatever it happens to be at any period, and to it the critics of the few news media that can make or break a play are also attuned. At present, the majority of customers, especially for the expensive seats, are out-of-towners on expense accounts. To them, these Broadway plays are what plays are supposed to be like; and, ironically, the plays tend to be made like what is supposed to appeal to these customers.

Costing less and less rule-ridden, off-Broadway can cover a wider and riskier spectrum of plays and style. And this was, of course, its purpose and justification when it made a splash ten years ago. Yet by and large, over the years, though it continues to produce more efficiently than Broadway, it has not continued to be much more artistically authentic, for it has gotten involved in the same interlocking complex. (See Appendix VI.) Most of its people are aspiring to Broadway success; they must woo the same critics, who treat them rather disdainfully; and in the end, to stay in business, off-Broadway relies for its main audience on New York career people, Ivy Leaguers, and rich suburbanites, a group more intellectual than the audience of Broadway, but neither ingenuous nor earnest nor artistic. Off-Broadway has become, ambiguously, the staging ground for those new things, writers, actors, foreign modern classics, that on their next time around will be highbrow on Broadway.

The change has been poignantly described by one of the chief off-Broadway producers, Ted Mann:

> Sure, we did our first plays at the Circle for $1,500, but it was a completely different sort of operation. No one got paid a penny of salary. We literally lived together, in the theater; we ate out of the communal pot. Everybody did everything. . . . The big change came when we decided to become more professional. We departmentalized. Actors just acted, directors just directed, porters just portered. If we hadn't done that, become more professional, off-Broadway would have died after the initial curiosity wore off.

Next, let us compare with these, two kinds of *nonprofit* theater. The first is the Official-Artistic, presenting high-standard repertory and supported by municipal or big-foundation money. This can be, at its worst, the crashingly pretentious Repertory Theater of Lincoln Center, whose real social costs are far beyond even Broadway. Or it can be a highly respectable regional center, like Tyrone Guthrie's new theater in

Minneapolis, with an endowment of three quarters of a million dollars and a theater costing two and a quarter million. The running budget for the first season: $660,-000 for twenty weeks. Such an enterprise is cost-comparable to an excellent museum or, as we shall see, to a Great University (and indeed Guthrie's theater is connected with the drama department of the University of Minnesota).

In startling contrast with all these is what might be called off-off-Broadway. These are plays and companies with entirely artistic or popular motivation, acting in a coffee shop or perhaps in the organ loft of a church. The people have learned from the degeneration of off-Broadway that it is impossible to get involved in the interlocking complex at all and remain authentic. One such company of artists, at the Judson Church in New York, spends $50 to $200 to mount a play and nothing at all to run it, since the script, actors, staff, and space are all given gratis by the like-minded. Yet in 1963-64 it was given the prize of the artistic critics (the *Village Voice* Toby) for providing the most interesting theater experiences of the year. But its small crowded audiences of friends can hardly be considered a public at all, and it rarely gets notices in the big news media.

Here is another possibility. The Living Theater (see Appendix VI), the liveliest off-Broadway venture, failed by declining to become "professional." Its present plan is to become a wandering community of actors in a caravan and play in schools, churches, village squares. Off-off-off-Broadway.

(In cinema, the ratio of costs is remarkably similar to those in theater. An unpretentious Class-A Hollywood movie might cost half a million to a million dollars. A high-level documentary, sponsored by a foundation, costs fifty to one hundred thousand. But one is more likely to win an international prize by spending two to five thousand dollars plus blood and tears, dreams and friends.)

4

Next, consider some contrasting costs in broadcasting.

A pretty good radio station in New York City, *e.g.* WMCA, charges $700 an hour to sponsor or advertise (this would not include the cost of any programs provided by the sponsor). WBAI, a non-profit and entirely independent station in New York of comparable range and audience, costs $38 an hour to run. It is supported by its listeners, with twelve thousand subscribers at $12 each, with the balance of the budget of $240,000 made up by contributions, friends, selling tapes, etc.

The paid staff of WBAI is twenty. Salary, top $12,000 down to $4,000. But besides, there are from ten to twenty-five irregular volunteers, mostly collegians, who do clerical and subscription work. Almost all the programming is provided gratis by well-known artists, academics, and political people of every persuasion who regard the station as an available outlet for themselves. But the small staff, scurrying with tape-recorders, also covers meetings and concerts and has made many remarkable documentaries. Besides, WBAI is one of the three independent stations of the Pacifica Foundation and exchanges tapes with the others. In 1964, in renewing the Pacifica licenses after a bitter fight—the stations were challenged as obscene and communistic—the FCC praised Pacifica as performing an outstanding public service and as being invaluable in combating the uniformity of most of broadcasting.

I am not acquainted with a TV outlet similar to radio WBAI; pay television is a commercial proposition. But the following three sets of comparative TV costs are instructive.

On the NBC network, sponsored time costs $143,000 an hour or $650 an outlet; and $2,000 an hour for a single station (New York). This does not include the cost of the program if provided by the sponsor.

(The cost of making TV programs by established methods is surprisingly high. A simple half-hour conversation with a guest and the showing of a few graphs is budgeted at $10,000. This comprises mainly rent and royalties for the studio and its patented devices; the usual featherbedding of stagehands to provide two chairs; technicians—*e.g.* twice $45 to work the needle on a phonograph; and a remarkable staff of artists, directors, editors, and producers who must be paid off. Big network documentaries may be budgeted at a quarter of a million. There is an anecdote of such a documentary portraying an impoverished area whose cost would have made the area flourish like a garden; and the film was scrapped without being shown.)

Now compare with the above, two non-profit TV stations, both members of National Educational TV, but widely different from each other in organization. WNDT, on the East Coast, costs more than $600 an hour to run (1963-64 budget, $2,900,000 for about 4,800 hours). This is not much cheaper than the selling price of time on the commercial network outlet, but of course it is only a third of the selling price for a single commercial station. (The WNDT figures include the cost of programming except for 10 per cent provided by NET.) The other non-profit station, however, KQED on the West Coast, runs for $225 an hour (1963-64, $540,000 for 2,400 hours). Professionally, the East Coast and the West Coast stations are equivalent, but the West Coast station is, in my opinion, rather more interesting. It makes daring, and inexpensive, use of live controversial meetings and is more alert to available personalities in the region. WNDT is more bogged down in "ideas" for series and in format panels.

WNDT is run like a top-drawer Institution, midway between Madison Avenue and a big university. Its top salary is $45,000. Its staff is about a hundred and fifty. The Western station is run by a band of artists, journalists, and technicians. Its top salary is $15,000 and the staff is about fifty. I have been told that the turnover of staff at KQED is practically nil, whereas its Eastern counterpart is largely a way station for persons moving toward higher salaries elsewhere.

Let me evaluate the three stations. WNDT, though never as disgusting, is usually duller than NBC. Dullness is a characteristic fault of the institutional noncommercial. KQED, however, is more interesting than NBC; it has neither to please everybody nor to protect an image; it can risk shaggy moments and hate-mail.

5

Next, some schools.

A prestigious but not fashionable non-residential private school in New York costs $850 per pupil per year, not counting plant and some endowment. Class size is about twenty. An elementary pupil in the New York public schools costs $700 per year, also excluding cost for plant, and the class size is about thirty-five. That is, public and private cost about the same. By contrast with both of these there is a Summerhill-type non-residential school with which I am acquainted that charges $450 a child; and, in this school, for fifty children there are three full-time paid instructors and the equivalent of five more voluntary teachers from among parents who are artists, craftsmen, or professionals. (In discussing the New York system, we saw that, despite tentative moves in the opposite direction, the more professional public and private schools discourage the entry of unlicensed teachers into the classroom.)

Whatever the pedagogic merits of this voluntary-teacher structure, in the school in question it has had drastic, perhaps predictable, organizational effects. The teachers and parent-teachers have ousted the founding headmaster, have run as a community-anarchy—with an equal vote for small children and confused adolescents!—have returned to a headmaster with limited authority, and so forth. But meantime the children have been exposed to many attentive knowledgeable adults and this, in my view, is a prime advantage. Other critics, however, might think all this is dreadful.

Next, let us invent a tiny prep school of sixty, run by a college, as Townsend Harris Hall was run by the College of the City of New York. By attending about three hours a day, the students will garner enough College Boards for college admission—and can have the rest of their time for more useful adolescent pursuits, whatever they happen to be. (Townsend Harris required five hours but for only three years and had many more courses than necessary for college admission.) The teachers are three willing graduate students of the university who would otherwise be hired as section-men or graders, at $3,000 (or less). Thus, the total expense of the tiny school for forty weeks is: $9,000 for teachers, $5,000 for a secretary, rent, and some equipment; at most, $300 per student. For bright and lively youngsters, this would obviously be a far more profitable and pleasant regimen than they get at almost any public high school at upwards of $1,000. (New York City,

$1,100.) Thus, if what is sought is good grades and college entrance, this is a direct and cheap way to get it.

College tuition, at Columbia or Cornell, is $1,700 a year, which is estimated to be a little more than 50 per cent of the actual cost per student for "education and educational administration," the rest being made up by endowment and grants. This is a steep markup of 400 per cent over actual classroom costs, for a professor's salary and customary rent. (At smaller liberal arts colleges of similar prestige the markup averages 300 per cent.) Yet the professors lecture to very big classes, especially in the freshman and sophomore years, and the smaller recitation and discussion classes are taught by section men who are very poorly paid. As I pointed out in *The Community of Scholars,* by returning to the pure academic tradition in which a university is a guild of professors or students or both, if the professors were paid the present national median for associate professor, the tuition per student would be only $650 (including middle-class rent), and there would be 10 professors for 150 students. The savings, in this model, are entirely due to elimination of administration and features aimed at aggrandizement.

In an actual experience of a guild of scholars, however, Black Mountain College, the total costs were indeed rather close to this model, but the breakdown was entirely different. During a period when Black Mountain attempted to operate without any endowment or contributions (1950), the total fee per student was $1,000 to $1,600, including tuition and room and board. Let us say that "tuition" was $700, about half of Columbia or Cornell's that year. There were eighteen faculty members for a hundred students. The faculty paid themselves varying sums from $600 to perhaps $2,000 a year, depending on family need, plus medical

insurance, food, and housing. The property belonged
to the faculty; the plant was largely constructed by the
students and faculty, and all shared in the work program. Thus, Black Mountain was more like an organic
"intentional" community than a university, and that
was in fact its tone and has been its influence in American culture.

6

The Peace Corps is known for its efficiency and dedicated administration, and it may serve us as an excellent type of highly centralized social service. The
American Friends run a somewhat comparable service,
VISA (Voluntary International Service Assignments),
which was, indeed, a model for the Peace Corps. Both
operations espouse the philosophy of "community development," the generation of self-help in the communities where they work; both are two-year programs
for volunteers; and both stress the educational value
for those who go abroad. But to repeat, accurate comparison is always impossible, because the methods and
the meaning are inextricably connected; and in the
present cases the comparative costs sharply reflect the
differences of methods and meaning.

The cost of selecting, training, and maintaining a
Peace Corps volunteer in the field for a year has been
about $14,000. (Estimating seven thousand volunteers
on a budget of $96,000,000. In 1964, the cost has been
cut to less than $12,000.) This includes $9,000 directly spent on the young person and $5,000 for cen-
tral administration in Washington, liaison with other
capitals, public relations, and so forth. These figures do
not include equipment and material used on the job,
which are provided under the general budget for foreign aid. The Friends program, by contrast, costs only
$3,500 a year, to select, train, and maintain a volunteer,

and to "administer" the program. Again the markup is our familiar 3-400 per cent. For very rough comparison, there is also another decentral program in this field, Operation Crossroads, on a summer-vacation (two-month) basis in Africa; prorated, the cost of Crossroads would be $5,000 per volunteer per year.

Why the difference in costs? In the first place, the Friends spend nothing at all on administration of this particular program. The program is small—fifty are involved in any one year—and it is administered at home and abroad as part of other Friends activities; it is just another willingly assumed burden. Generally speaking, too, the Friends work for little more than subsistence anyway. Secondly, the criteria and expenses of selection are entirely different. The Peace Corps is, and is meant to be, an Image; therefore nothing must go wrong; every volunteer must be carefully checked and cleared. Only one of eight original applicants is finally sent abroad. Also, the projects are highly pre-planned and very specific skills are sought for. By and large, only college graduates or even postgraduates are acceptable. (This works out, let me say, to making the Corps an upper-middle-class operation. Poor youth rarely qualify, and middle-class youth on the make cannot afford to "waste" two years.) These stringent requirements do not necessarily make much sense, however, for in many cases, perhaps the majority, the actual job proves to have little relation to the specific qualifications or the specific training; field conditions are not predictable, or have rapidly changed. The Friends seem to take this more for granted and their criteria for selection are more simply relevant: health, desire to serve, ability to cooperate in stress. Those who volunteer for Friends' service are pretty surely committed beforehand to a service philosophy. But the Peace Corps makes a glamorous mass appeal and must then weed out the numbers that apply—nor is its own philosophy without ambiguity. (I am at a loss as to why the Peace Corps is not under the United Nations.) Thirdly, Peace Corps training, in languages, technical skill, history, politics, and ideology is done in an American university setting by highly paid professors, with plenty of testing and observation by expensive psychologists. The Friends consider that some of this is unnecessary—most natives in "backward" countries have not heard of Russia *or* America—and that some of it is better taught in the field by native teachers. (As Flo Weinberger has pointed out in a study of Peace Corps and VISA, there is an ironical contradiction in community development, which is decentralist by nature, being governed by distant bureaucratic considerations.)

Thus, at least some of the extra costs of the Peace Corps are due to its peculiar and incommensurate requirements. Yet my hunch is that a good many are also due to the attitudes, departmentalization, and salaries of all big official organizations. For example, a small pilot project of the so-called Domestic Peace Corps in Harlem managed to use $250,000 to train and place thirty volunteers, or $8,500 a head, even without boat fare, touchy international image, special training in languages, and highly selective requirements. There has been hot criticism of inefficient administration and excessive amounts of "research" in the Harlem project; but these too are usual in centralized operations.

I am told (December 1964) that the Peace Corps is now remedying some of the traits of its first years. Most important, it is realized that many of its services can equally well be performed by right-spirited slum youth or farm youth, and the attempt will be made to recruit these without the forbidding application forms. Psychologizing and investigation are being somewhat diminished; the ratio of rejection is now six to one and should fall further. Training can be carried on in less pretentious settings, more similar to actual field conditions. (Mississippi?) Now that the framework is established, administrative costs should continue to fall somewhat. Overseas administration is being decentralized, and more and more of the staffing will consist of returnees, who are strongly motivated. I trust all this will come to pass.

7

Finally, let me compare the costs in two housing schemes for the same city neighborhood.

The first is the proposal for the west side of Greenwich Village prepared by the New York City Housing and Redevelopment Board, as Urban Renewal. This proposal met fierce neighborhood resistance, led by a group of intellectuals with press backing. To qualify for renewal, the neighborhood had been certified as technically a slum, but in most important ways it was not a slum. The proposal was for massive demolition, dislocating most of the area's population and destroying many small businesses. The plan for reconstruction called for the usual bureaucratically designed tall buildings which, the neighborhood felt, were unnecessary and out of keeping. Managing to stall the Housing Board's proposal, the organized neighborhood then offered a counter-plan, on the principles of dislocating no one except by choice, of demolishing as little as possible that was salvageable, and of tailor-making an artistic design for the community. (Both plans are still only proposals.)

The cost of the Urban Renewal scheme would be $30,000,000 and would, after demolition and relocation, provide a net increase of 300 dwelling units. The cost of the Neighborhood scheme would be $8,500,000 and would provide, with no relocation, 475 new dwelling units. (Since New York City has long had an absolute shortage of housing, the avoidance of relocation is itself a great advantage, apart from the question of neighborhood disruption.)

Again, the great discrepancy in economic and social costs in the two schemes is implicit in their organizational methods and attitudes. The efficient bureaucrat tries to provide a large number of units as cheaply as possible and uses a standard approach and design, but tends to overlook the concrete local situation and also the big context of the need of the whole city. All dwellings that do not conform to an abstract standard of life are considered substandard, unlivable, demolishable. Administratively, it would be too much trouble to pick and choose among old houses—especially since the thorny legal business of evictions falls to another department. (And needless to say, from the promoter's point of view, there is money to be made in demolition as well as construction.) What is the consequence of this demolition-and-standard-construction approach? If the particular purpose is to house the poor, a poor ghetto is created; if middle-class, a middle-class ghetto; and if social pressures require that some of the dislocated poor be rehoused in the project, both kinds of ghetto are juxtaposed with maximum invidious effect. Housing is treated like any other mass-produced commodity, although, as I have pointed out, in the actual construction many advantages of mass production are neglected.

The other scheme, on the contrary, cares about the existing neighborhood. It is the particular neighborhood that is to be improved, rather than providing housing in the abstract or clearing an abstract slum. The method, therefore, is to conserve population, established businesses, and buildings. This saves money.

And since the construction is on a more modest scale, a cheaper mode of construction can be used. (But this kind of problem then arises: bare brick is specified for some interior walls, both because it is cheaper and the architect likes the texture, which indeed he uses in his own home. This is against an Ordinance that requires plaster. Fifty years ago, plaster, rather than wallpaper, would have been considered outrageous.) Very striking is the fact that the proposal, which must have required hundreds of hours of work by many professionals, cost only $3,500 to prepare; this would be a few months' salary for one draftsman in a bureaucratic office.

Nevertheless, just as in discussing Broadway and off-Broadway, we found that off off-Broadway there was a still simpler economic scale, so we must notice that in this very neighborhood many a pleasant dwelling has already been saved from slum by means even cheaper than the West Village Neighborhood plan. The units of the West Village plan come to $18,000 apiece; but it has been possible in this neighborhood to rent space much cheaper (estimating twenty years' amortization), and to renovate it and make it charming with $500 to $1,000 worth of materials plus the labor and skill of oneself and one's friends. This is the background of the persistent hassle in New York about the artists' lofts. Artists take over cold-water flats and commercial slums and remodel them. Naturally this does nothing for the tax base and the city is glad to cooperate with promoters who, by evictions, can collect parcels of real estate. The artists' lofts are called substandard firetraps, and are condemned. Yet it is not evident that by this process better housing is provided cheaper.

8

To sum up: What swell the costs in enterprises carried on in the interlocking centralized systems of society, whether commercial, official, or non-profit institutional, are all the factors of organization, procedure, and motivation that are not directly determined to the function and to the desire to perform it. These are patents and rents, fixed prices, union scales, featherbedding, fringe benefits, status salaries, expense accounts, proliferating administration, paper work, permanent overhead, public relations and promotion, waste of time and skill by departmentalizing task-roles, bureaucratic thinking that is penny-wise pound-foolish, inflexible procedure and tight scheduling that exaggerate contingencies and overtime.

But when enterprises can be carried on autonomously by professionals, artists, and workmen intrinsically committed to the job, there are economies all along the line. People make do on means. They spend on value, not convention. They flexibly improvise procedures as opportunity presents and they step in in emergencies. They do not watch the clock. The available skills of each person are put to use. They eschew status and in a pinch accept subsistence wages. Administration and overhead are *ad hoc*. The task is likely to be seen in its essence rather than abstractly.

We have seen that in an assortment of service enterprises, intrinsic procedures can regularly be cheaper by three, five, and ten times—and, of course, indefinitely cheaper if people simply want to do a job and are not supporting themselves by it at all.

It does not follow, however, that we ought to think of voluntary production and distribution as an ideal, as in William Morris' lovely romance, *News from Nowhere*. In my opinion, there are many valid moral and psychological objections to it as a general formula—I shall list some of them at the beginning of the next chapter; paradoxically, it is *over*-strenuous and *over*-earnest. My conclusion is, rather, that we ought to aim at a mixed system with, at present, more decentralism than we have.

9

An interesting result of our little collection of comparative costs is the surprising emergence of a kind of Typology of Enterprises for a mixed system. There appear four well-marked classes. (To make a rounded theory, we shall immediately add three others.)

A. Enterprises extrinsically motivated and interlocked with the other centralized systems.

> *1. Run primarily for profit.*
> *E.g.* Broadway theater, NBC.

(I have not bothered to explore the costs of commercial enterprises in the other functions dealt with in this chapter, *e.g.* commercial housing or the maintenance by Standard Oil of a crew in Venezuela.)

> *2. Institutional Non-profit.*
> *E.g.* Civic theater, WNDT, Public School System, Big University, Peace Corps, Urban Renewal.

B. Enterprises intrinsically motivated and tailored to the concrete product or service.

> *1. Professional and Craft.*
> *E.g.* Off-Broadway, KQED, Settlement House Social Work, West Village Neighborhood housing.
> *2. Purely Artistic or Community.*
> *E.g.* Off off-Broadway, Pacifica Radio, Black Mountain College, Friends Service, Artists' lofts.

In principle, in a period of semi-monopoly, Class A-1., the centralized profit enterprises, ought to be the most costly, since everybody involved is out to make the most money possible, whether profits, salary, or wages. But in fact, institutional or official non-profit enterprises might be more or less costly, for status salaries and expense accounts are equally prevalent, excessive administration and overhead are often more prevalent, and there is less pressure to trim costs. This typology usefully cuts across the usual division of profit and non-profit (*e.g.* capitalism *vs.* socialism).

Ideally, in a highly centralized society, profit and non-profit enterprises provide a salutary check on each other, as the TVA is supposed to provide a yardstick for the price of electricity. In fact, we have generally been getting the *coalition* of Classes A-1. and A-2.—the industrial-military complex; the alliance of promoters, contractors, and government in Urban Renewal; the alliance of universities, corporations, and government in research and development. This is the great domain of cost-plus. Profit enterprises can proceed with all the expensive perquisites and dignity of non-profit enterprises, and also tack on a profit.

It is an historical curiosity that Class B-1., autonomous professional and craft groups who are *not* out to make a big profit, is our nearest contemporary equivalent to Adam Smith's model of the Entrepreneur. The primary interest of a classical entrepreneur was to produce useful goods and make enough profit to stay in business and enterprise further. (Whether or not this was his conscious intention, the laws of the market were supposed to guarantee that this would be his behavior.)

This continuity of the enterprise is the essential difference between Classes B-1. and B-2., between the professional and the artistic or community enterprises that tend to be *ad hoc,* satisfying an impulse or inspiration or meeting a pressing need that arises. For a continuously productive artist or a compassionate social worker, each work or case is really *ad hoc.* But professionals require a more permanent framework in which they can keep practicing their professions. Besides, they are members of a guild or peer group, and this sets extrinsic standards of status-salary and perquisites, which are reflected in the rather stable professional costs, whereas artistic costs can fluctuate wildly.

Yet there is more social continuity in artistic production than would seem possible, but it does not reside in a continuous "enterprise." For instance, a little magazine is likely to lapse after two issues; yet another little magazine will at once spring up with a different masthead and different financing but almost exactly the same authors. This is because everybody knows everybody and all are somewhat after the same thing.

Inevitably, the most wildly fluctuating prices, if not costs, are in the coalition of A-1. and B-2., commercial impresario with artist. For here we have the rarity of the unique with the promotion and motivation of the mass market. Thus, artists may make extraordinary amounts of money for what, under other conditions, they just as willingly do for nothing.

10

At the extreme limit of costly enterprises is the always potentially important class that we described in the last chapter: bureaucracies that "run for their own sake." They are infinitely expensive in the sense that they are supported by society and produce no products at all. Let us call them Class A-o.

Their products are, of course, symbolical. They are the turning Tibetan prayer wheels which signify that everything is in order. We saw that public school systems can approximate this role. The stock exchange and other privately operated gambling establishments are similar. And no doubt, much of government. But it must also be said that, in the end, the widely accepted concept of expanding the economy primarily in order to reduce unemployment is just such a running of a system for its own sake. People work to keep the economic system in operation and the system operates in order to keep people working. This is not funny.

And at the other extreme, even less costly than the highly efficient but sporadic artistic and community system of enterprise, is the utterly decentralized production and servicing that is done by families and individuals for themselves, and by friends, folk, and amateurs. Even in our market society, this kind no doubt still produces the majority of valuable goods and services, *e.g.* housekeeping, home cooking, child rearing, shaving oneself, friendly games and parties, affectionate sex, hobbies, etc. But in all such, the chief value is outside the cash nexus (itemized, for instance, on a hotel bill), and it is not much considered a proper subject of economic analysis. (The last extensive treatment I know is Borsodi's *Prosperity and Security*.)

In my opinion, however, just the *relations* of such "non-economic" production and consumption with the various cost systems give us a powerful index of social and economic health. A rational economist must finally be concerned with how well people live, not with what things cost. In measuring the wealth of society, it is absurd to rely entirely on the Gross National Product, for much of it may be worse than useless. It is important to notice how much the various expensive products and services of corporations and government make people subject to repairmen, fees, commuting, queues, unnecessary work, dressing just for the job; and these things often prevent satisfaction altogether.

The type case, mentioned by Galbraith, is the man taking aspirin as the car radiator boils over in the traffic jam on the way to the overcrowded public beach: every part of this is good for the Gross National Product and will be subsumed under Recreation. Similarly, in measuring the contribution to society of the arts, professions, and communications, it is important to notice how they effect the quality, taste, and intelligence of people, and what people then do for themselves. Are they mere time-killing, if not worse? In this respect, pretentious Art Centers like Lincoln Square probably do far more harm than good. They create in the public the impression that what they present *is* genuine modern art, and honest youngsters are then discouraged. Rather, official money should stick to underwriting *museum* art, theater, and opera, and provide that new artists can live in *decent* poverty.

11

Finally, there is the great class of enterprises that provide for essential public needs that are the background for all other functions. Since these needs are essential and universal, it is probably wisest not to think of them in terms of cost at all. Let us call them Class C. In this class, the productive motivations that are relevant are professional efficiency and ethics and citizenly service. These are tasks to be attended to with reliability, honesty, and skill; certainly not competitively, and not necessarily creatively.

In a complicated modern society, such background necessities cover an enormous range: mass transportation, mail, telephone, electric power, pavement, water supply, museums, recreation areas, literacy, public health, standard information, etc., etc. It is impossible to think of a modern community without these. In the case of some of them, their special non-economic nature is signalized by free appropriation (*e.g.* pavement, museums); in other cases by non-economic prices (*e.g.* mail, literacy). In the long run, it would probably be simpler, more efficient, and cheaper to provide them *all* gratis. *E.g.* "When all the new electronic machinery is in place . . . the cost of preparation of itemized phone bills may be greater than the cost of providing the service." (Asher Brynes.)

Robert Theobald and the other economists of the Triple Revolution believe that, in the state of present technology, we should pay for decent minimum subsistence in the same category, rather than assigning it to "welfare." I agree with this, but I am still persuaded, as in Scheme III of *Communitas*, that a large proportion of decent subsistence could be provided with most security and least cost by direct production in a separate sector, outside of the cash nexus. Automation adds a strong confirmation of this point of view. (I will return to these points later.)

12

In various proportions, every modern society probably has all these seven types of enterprise. What would constitute a "mixed system" is the proportionate weighting of the types, to be an effective pluralism: so that they usefully influence and enhance one another and, if necessary, can check one another. This relative weighting of actual functions, with contrasting interest groups, is the *real* constitution, as Aristotle said. Thus, the United States, the Soviet Union, Sweden, Nigeria, etc., have different constitutions, and the real constitution of the United States is continually changing. (Jefferson implied that the written constitution therefore should be periodically overhauled.)

But also for cost efficiency, for any set of technological and social conditions, there is probably a rough optimum proportion of types of enterprise, or better, limits of unbalance beyond which the system gives sharply diminishing returns. A mixed system would remain within the efficient range. But I doubt very much that at present the United States is in this efficient range. We seem to put an inordinate expense into maintaining the structure. Everywhere one turns—not only in the kinds of cases in this chapter—there seems to be a markup of 300 and 400 per cent, to do anything or make anything. This is an intolerable drag.

Consider it simply this way: One visits a country where the per capita income is one quarter of the American, but, lo and behold, these unaffluent people do *not* seem four times "worse off" than we, or hardly worse off at all. Do the Irish live only a fourth as well as we? Or again, it takes $30,000 in new investment to re-employ one unemployed workman. When this amount of new investment is unavailable or pointless, we assign the person to the slag heap—supported by social insurance—but we do not think of modifying the conditions of enterprise. Or add up the costs in agencies, police, extra school services, etc., to maintain one family in poverty and anomie—a group at Columbia has estimated that it would pay the city to give the family $10,000 to get out of town! There *might* be several more cost-efficient arrangements. And on the other hand, as we shall see, there are public goods and services that are useful and even necessary but that—with the present arrangements—we "cannot afford."

Let me list the areas that we have noticed where excessive centralization might be grossly expensive:

1. Where staff and overhead are the chief costs. These are the social, personal, and artistic services, like those mainly dealt with in this chapter.

2. Where the cost of distribution or servicing out-weighs the savings in centralized production. The type function is the farm and food business, as described in Chapter III. But probably more important than these areas, where the losses can be traced and somewhat measured, are the areas of hidden costs or subsidiary damages that are paid for under different headings where they are not ordinarily traced.

3. Where central planning and rationalization go beyond the flowing changes and contingencies of life and lead to overcommitment and inflexibility. To give an immensely important present case: we use computers to give speedy feedback and flexibility of adjustment but, ironically, if the "goals" of a long-range program have been set, the programming may produce, instead, a monstrous inflexibility. Donald Michael has put this well:

> Whatever the nature of a long-range program, once priorities are assigned and the physical, manpower, and psychological resources of the nation are committed, it will take close to catastrophic revisions in reality or exceptional conviction by the highest national leadership to make it politically worthwhile to shift these commitments. The success or failure of a program may take years to determine. Until then, a strong bureaucratic and industrial constituency which benefits from the program is unlikely to be replaced except by extraordinarily compelling needs to revise priorities. The more interlocked the parts, the more powerful the parts, the more difficult it will be to get all the parts to move in another direction. [Commencement Address, Marlboro College, 1964.]

Thus, Israel was long saddled with a concrete-and-glass architecture that did not suit the climate and conditions; millions died in Russia because of a centralized agricultural program which happened to be inept, and so forth.

4. Where the departmentalization and standardization, which miss the uniqueness of each person, produce imbalances and positive damage that must then be expensively remedied. *E.g.* an inept system of schooling, skimping on teachers and personal attention, creates misfits who are then processed, at $2,000 a year, in a reform school; and this is just the beginning of the social costs.

The present centralist philosophy, therefore, is to have "comprehensive" social programs which will account in a balanced way for all aspects, as in the War on Poverty. Such an integrated approach is intelligent; but when it is aggrandized and standardized, it inevitably covers the whole of life and no escape but resignation. As Edgar and Jean Cahn have pointed out in a grimly humorous study of the comprehensive Human Renewal program in New Haven, the program becomes a War indeed, "fought by professionals on behalf of the civilian population. They mobilize by creating a monopoly over the engines of war," for instance by incorporating the settlement houses. "They launch an offensive by the establishment of multiple donor-donee relationships. . . . A strategy is mapped out by the military to minimize casualties to the military." The result is a permanent army of occupation, which is expensive.

CHAPTER VI

Personnel and Persons

1

Nevertheless, even within wide limits, cost efficiency is in general not a big deal at present. The savings involved in the small-scale and intrinsic style, as described in the preceding chapter, happen to be crucial in sensitive areas like education, social work, radio and theater, where there is need to experiment, to pay close attention to concrete cases, to risk being unpopular. But ours is not an economy of scarcity. A better proportioned system would be more efficient, but we do not need to be all that efficient. We can spend a vast amount of money, material, and effort on markup, on the structure, on being proud of one's income even if one can't take it home, and yet still have an increasing number of goods and services. The vital questions that are raised by analyzing costs are moral, psychological, and political.

They are not simple or one-sided questions. Wastefulness and squandering are not necessarily evil. They are, in a sense, our birthright. Our present productivity is the result of the accumulated labor of generations and the ingenuity and inventiveness of mankind. Folly and waste—advertising, Parkinson's Law, expense accounts, installment buying—are not new or fatal vices. Long ago Mandeville pointed out that private vices were public benefits. At least within the United States, if we could solve the political and social hang-ups, we would have no poverty; and if everybody has enough, it doesn't much matter if some operators get a disproportionate share.

Besides, the centralized and bureaucratic style has important moral advantages. We have seen that pedantic due process and red tape often make for fairness. Workmen who are not engaged in their own intrinsic enterprises, whether in capitalist or state-socialist societies, must protect themselves by union scales and even featherbedding. Status salaries pay not for the job but for the entire career, *e.g.* long schooling or seniority, so they are a means of structuring and justifying one's life. Many who are only semi-skilled probably work best and happiest in a framework of standard procedures. In many functions, there is less psychological and social wear and tear in carrying on in a routine and established setting, with permanent bureaucracy and overhead, even though this is less efficient for any particular performance. And rents, royalties, patents, profits, and the cash nexus in general would not be an implausible fabric of society if they could be strictly limited in their power to sabotage excellence and to do injustice, and if they could be regarded with more, so to speak, humor than we are accustomed.

Also, if a society can at all afford it, there is great political virtue in providing many pleasant quasi sine-cures, especially for the old, to keep them in the stream of useful social life. Oddly, we seem to have hit on such a thing rather for the young, "going to college," and this would be acceptable, except that we have Calvinistically set it up so that the experience is not nearly so pleasant as it might be: we make the young waste their time with their noses to the grindstone.

2

But the bother with our style is the general phoniness and slovenliness that spread from the inflated and inefficient economy. There is a lot of pretentious busywork, but useful things are skimped and cut back in order to invest in more profitable stupidities. It is sickening to see, on TV, the news of poverty and riot intermitted with the ads. Essential needs that promise no profits are neglected altogether. Hard-core poverty is not a mere accident in an affluent society; it would not exist in a rich society. Deliberately or unwittingly, the proliferation of standard goods that are easy to sell destroys simpler satisfactions. And, not least, there is a venal abuse of scientific research and technical development. It is sad that the austere nineteenth-century vision of a scientific way of life, the vision of Thomas Huxley and Veblen, should come to this.

All this is inevitable when persons are not *engaged* in what they are doing and don't really know what it's about or what they're about, when the initiative and invention of talented or sensible people are balked because too much capital and social machinery have to be set in motion to do anything; when the standard products are inauthentic; and when the official speech is not true.

In this chapter let us take up again the difference between being personnel and being a person. For whether or not one shares my dim view of the present scene, the question is a crucial one, namely, Is our

society humanly possible—especially with the maturing
of automation? The terminus of being personnel is
1984.

3

If we collect recent uses of the concept "Personnel,"
it seems to mean those who man any kind of organization. But we can see the essence by consulting an older
dictionary: *Personnel* is "the body of persons employed in a public service, as the army or navy, as opposed to the *matériel*." Here the emphasis is on the
personification of the organization, *e.g.* it is a striking
force with a unitary will of its own; the persons are
part of its means, along with the material means.

In the army, everyone from private to general is
personnel, and people are completely defined by their
grade and role in the organization; but the President,
the commander in chief, would not be called personnel. In a hospital, by contrast, the doctors are not personnel; they are defined by oath and peer group outside the organization. But orderlies, nurses, and interns
are personnel. What about the patients? Historically,
they are not personnel but personal clients of the doctors. Consider, however, the hospital studied (with grim
humor) by Rose Laub Coser, where the nurses complain that the patients are too much on the move; what
they would prefer is "one patient permanently in one
bed"—this would save time and work for everybody,
it would be administratively more convenient. The patients would then be personnel.

In a university the professors are not yet personnel.
Historically, of course, the guild of professors *was* the
universitas, or corporation; but at present the administration has become the university, and includes not
only the office staff and groundkeepers but the counselors, coaches, admissions directors, examiners, and

deans who have taken over many of the functions that
belonged to faculty; all these are personnel. In this
change, curiously, the students have not tended to be
incorporated into personnel, except for the student
government; they have rather become *matériel*, for
processing.

In the New York public school system, on the other
hand, teachers are personnel, are examined, hired, and
fired by the associate superintendent for personnel.

Congressmen are not personnel. Up to now, the
members of a ball team have not been personnel. They
play ball because they like to, and a team in a game is a
voluntary association. But the announced policy of the
Yankee front office is more businesslike and regards
the farm system and the team as personnel. (*E.g.* at the
time of the purchase by CBS, Yogi Berra was assured
that there would be "no changes in personnel.") I
doubt that this policy is feasible, however, for both as
athletes and as entertainers the players must be ultimately direct and spontaneous, they must play ball
rather than carry on the goal of the organization.

In a business or industrial corporation, the members
of the board and the president are not personnel. (The
stockholders have become simply pensioners of the
system.) But junior executives are management-
personnel, salesmen are sales-personnel, assembly-line
workers are production-personnel, etc. An inventor or
designer, however, even if he is on a salary rather than
free lancing, is probably not hired and scheduled as
personnel.

The unemployed are, generally, best regarded as clients of the professional welfare agencies. But there are
interesting signs of making them personnel, as "sub-
professionals." For instance, in a job-retraining program, the new skill that a man learns might be outmoded before he has finished training, and this might

happen three or four times; but then he becomes a
teacher of retraining, personnel. Similarly, the best
prognosis for a convict on probation is for him to gravitate to becoming a deputy probation officer, police-
personnel.

Seriously—though it is hard not to smile—this is not
bad social therapy and psychotherapy; it is the method
of the Halfway House, that provides security and
schedule and also gives opportunity for re-integration
into the community. Surprisingly, the administration
itself becomes the Halfway House. The other side of
the coin is that, in urban society, it is necessary to become a case of some kind in order to be paid attention
as a human being. Only clients are people, and one
graduates from client to personnel.

4

As our society becomes disposed to increase the
number of personnel and clients of professional-
personnel, there is a change also in the concept of
"professional."

From medieval times, a professional—typically,
physician or lawyer—was an artist in that he dealt with
individual cases, each one unique. A physician treats a
patient, not a pathology or syndrome. He himself is
therefore engaged as a person, not merely as a scientist;
he is bound by a special ethical code, and he is personally licensed by the Sovereign and by his peers' acceptance of him as a peer. (In medieval times, the doctors
of the university recommended his licensing to the
Sovereign and the Sovereign had to comply.)

At present, the status of physician and lawyer is essentially unchanged. The clergy has either succumbed
to administration or, in some cases, has become entirely maverick and personal, no longer a profession.
Some architects continue like old-fashioned profes-

sionals. But there is a proliferation of other new professionals whose status is quite different, *e.g.* social workers, school teachers, various business consultants. In actuality, these are licensed when they pass standard examinations and fulfill other standard requirements of courses and credits; and the concept of them is not that they are artists, but that they have a body of knowledge which they can apply to the range of cases that they are "qualified" to deal with. In most actual cases of social worker, nurse, engineer, etc., the professional is not in a one-to-one correspondence with his client but is employed by an organization to operate over a range of cases and within rather well-defined limits of decision. It is the organization, not the professional, that has final responsibility. The professional cannot fundamentally criticize the procedure without quitting the organization.

Whatever its advantages, this arrangement can be unfortunate for both the professional and the organization. It invites the professional to play it safe for organizational reasons rather than professional prudence; to follow the routine rather than the uniquely appropriate procedure; and perhaps to be a time-server. And such an organizational role becomes one's whole career, takes up one's time of life. For example, a fine architect, who works in a big office, was commissioned to build a major monumental building. He would not have gotten this commission except as a member of the firm; yet as a member of the firm, he is so pressed with work that he can give only a few months to the design of this important building that should have taken a couple of years of devoted study. The building looks it.

Let me quote a melancholy paragraph of Carl Stover of Stanford: "Anyone who has been part of the Federal service has seen too many eager, talented youngsters blighted by the system to be sanguine about whether it truly nurtures the best in men. Too frequently, breaking a man to the Federal 'harness' also breaks his spirit. By mid-career, many have all but lost their capacity for intellectual and spiritual growth as a result of serving as functionaries in a complex bureaucracy. They are dying from the top down, and there is little at work in the system to prevent it."

On the other hand, an organization can become bogged down by having to conform to irrelevant "professional standards" determined by distant Regents. For instance, an autonomous settlement house cannot hire an unlicensed worker from the neighborhood because it must maintain "professional standards" to get its city subsidy. And plenty of the new "professions" are rackets. There are diplomas, but there is not in fact any body of knowledge in the field, or tradition of personal responsibility, that could properly be called professional.

Worst of all, the clients of professional-personnel become themselves standard units, clients of the agency and subject to its schedule, paper forms, and criteria. It has happened that a person in need of help, and whom independent professionals would take on as a matter of course, is vainly sent from one agency to another because his circumstances are eccentric. No one is "qualified" to deal with just this case; for legal reasons no agency can take the responsibility. Again, in the cases of school building and public housing we have seen what bureaucratic professional design can amount to, and it is no different in big "private" offices.

Needless to say, from the status of client-personnel it is a short step to becoming a permanent client, generation after generation, for this is a role like any other.

5

A craftsman, mechanic, or technician is engaged, is *in* his job, in several ways: by his style, skill, and science in the process, which make him indispensable; and because the product is useful and he is needed in the community. He becomes personnel when the style and skill are built into the machine that he operates; when he no longer understands the process as a whole and does not decide the method and schedule; and when he has no control over the utility or price of the product, nor over his own hiring and firing. Then he is just a hand.

Correspondingly, there have been several kinds of relevant opposition to the "alienation" of labor. Arts-and-craftsmen have objected to standardized production altogether, as robbing the workman of style. Syndicalists have objected to losing control of the process and product. The conventional and Marxist labor movements, we have seen, have tended rather to increase centralization and alienation, though making it less intolerable.

Luddite, machine-breaking movements are a peculiar confusion of different kinds of complaint. Naturally, with automation, they have started up again. Being put out of work by new machines, Luddites see the machines themselves as inhuman. My impression is that true arts-and-craftsmen are more likely to admire the elegance, ingenuity, and accuracy of new machines, and to use them when possible. Frank Lloyd Wright is a good example; his aim was to make non-standard houses with honestly machined surfaces. "William Morris' hatred of machines," said Kropotkin, "proved that the conception of the machine's gracefulness was missing from his poetical genius." And of course the sober moral judgment of any workman is to use the most efficient tool; anything else is degrading. I doubt that there have ever been Luddites with good consciences.

Historically, the engagement of craftsman and professional was analogous. A craftsman was accepted into the guild of his peers by making a masterpiece and, just as with a professional, this achievement signalized a long growth, by apprenticeship, into a career that had become second nature. Usually he would have a prior disposition to the craft, by family, or locality, or personal talent. Thus, induction into a job was a process of personal engagement, not unlike the doctor's ring and kiss. It must be said, however, that unlike the humane professions, attachment to a craft or mechanic trade could easily produce a craft-idiot or drudge. Up to a point, "alienation" from this situation was liberating, both from narrow ideas and long hours.

But at present, such work has no relation whatever to what a man is or has become. The job gives no identity at all; and finally even the class, "being a working-man," gives no solidarity—one might as well be paid for featherbedding or unemployment. Typically, it takes six weeks to break in an average worker, three weeks if the plant is highly automated, and this on the basis of no prior training or schooling. And getting the job, especially for a poor youth who cannot look around, is not a matter of taste, choice, or background, but simply of making a living.

Nevertheless, there is a great noise about the need for long years of schooling in order to fit into the economy. Youth are warned not to drop out of high school or they will not have the skills required for employment. I am afraid that for most poor youth, and the jobs they will get, this is a hoax. The evident purpose of the schooling is baby-sitting and policing, during a period of excessive urbanization and youth unemployment. The only relevant skill that is taught in school is to be personnel: punctual and well-behaved. The "functional illiteracy" that is so much talked about has no relation to reading for truth, beauty, or citizenship but is *entirely* training to read directions and be personnel. When there is no industry in which to be personnel, one becomes client-personnel of the professional-personnel.

6

There is a duality, and always a potential contradiction, in being personnel. On the one hand, one does a job or confronts a client; on the other, one staffs the Organization. In ideal management theory, no such contradiction need arise, for the organization is supposed to be designed to satisfy every case. But the probability is overwhelming that, in a complex organization, a staff member will be forced to act unprofessionally, and precisely such action will be regarded as "professional." I have mentioned the case of the schoolteacher in a tizzy about the chewing gum because of the possible descent of the supervisor; or conversely, the architect who "unprofessionally" will not tear down a fine building. In *The Community of Scholars*, I mentioned another important kind of case: medical students ambitious for licensing are not interested in niceties of scientific analysis or thoroughgoing diagnosis; they want the professor to concentrate on the "meat" of the course, namely, what is necessary for the examination.

Professionals act ethically because of a quasi-religious commitment to the spirit of the profession; and they can be judged only by peers consulting their own empathetic response to the concrete situation. Craftsmen have an instinct of workmanship and are judged by the product and the guild. But professional-personnel are judged by adherence to the correct procedure, and production-personnel by the standard of a "fair day's work for a fair day's pay," where the equity is determined entirely by a contract negotiated by labor bureaucrats.

I would suggest that it is to avoid just this theoretical contradiction, in a society that has become largely centralized, that academic sociologists have come to lay such astonishing stress on the concept of "Role." Role is the *internalizing* of the duties and status that belong to personnel. It is Role, rather than medicine, jurisprudence, craft, labor, or science, that now becomes second nature. And, of course, once the organizational demands are internalized, there is no further "personal" conflict.

Frankly, except as an explanation to fit the realities of capitalist or state-socialist societies, I am baffled at the global significance that sociologists attach to Role. (Maybe I don't get the point.) Role-playing is an important part of neurotic conformity, equivalent to the Jungian *persona;* and it is a part of normal identification, like putting on a uniform. But these sociologists seem to explain all social behavior as a self-enclosed system of playing roles for one another's expectations. In these explanations, there is an uncanny neglect of animality and passion, of invention and technique, liberty and community, rational choice of objective values, history, and, indeed, experience of a real world at all. But if these factors are irrelevant, how shall we survive, not to speak of changing anything?

7

To sum up the argument of this book, let us review the broad facts of our social life during the second Industrial Revolution. Their inescapable meaning is that we are artificing a social machine running for its own aggrandizement, in which all citizens are personnel. (Unless, as is likely, an historical catastrophe knocks our course awry.)

By now, technological improvement and mass production could have resulted in a simplification of life, general security, and an increase in choice and liberty. They would have done so if they had been directed primarily to provide basic necessities, standard conveniences, and routine services. When they have been so directed, they have eliminated absolute privation, have nearly eliminated epidemic and infantile diseases, and have multiplied useful goods.

But abused, they have been a means of creating artificial complication in every sphere of life, general insecurity, competition heightened to the point of anxiety, and regimentation. In some respects production has been unplanned and there have been both duplication and neglect; but mainly, it has been planned for irrelevant reasons, to produce too many of too many kinds of commodities and to create a synthetic demand for them. The concentration of control in too few minds has sapped intelligence and independence and has fragmented voluntary associations and communities. The interlocking of parts is so inflexible that unless all enterprises run at a good speed, it is impossible to produce and distribute bread.

Economically, those who are not needed as personnel for this system have no productive life at all and inevitably become out-caste. The number of these increases, for in the new Industrial Revolution the exploitation of labor is not a major factor in production. According to various estimates, at the present stage of automation, twenty to forty thousand are thrown out every week. A RAND estimate is that the present goods and services can finally be produced by 2 per cent of the present labor force.

But politically, these out-caste and unemployed must be coped with. And the consensus of all politicians is to cope by expanding the Gross National Product by new investment, production, and sales; and to retrain the out-caste so they can contribute to the expansion. Expansion will solve all problems: increase profits, give jobs and allay unrest, and raise the standard of living. Even public goods, that have been shamefully neglected, are mentioned favorably.

It is impossible to regard this desperate policy without repugnance. (And obviously, if the RAND estimate is correct, it is a chimera.) Every part of it is a lifeless abstraction. The transactions that measure the GNP can be anything at all, so long as money changes hands and the shelves are cleared. Employment means keeping people busy. Education means training in a marketable skill. And what shall we say of a standard of living that boomed as a petty-bourgeois emulation of conspicuous consumption and is now also synthetic?

Economists might say it is a matter of taste; human beings have an infinite appetite for economic goods. Have they? Such an idea is strongly against common sense and rational political economy. It is possible that the appetite for experience and growth is infinite, but not the appetite for commodities bought at an American market.

The expanding GNP is the bathos of the once earnest and adventurous middle class.

But the worst is that the entrapment, the tight interlocking of all parts, now becomes a deliberate policy. Consider the encroachment of big government that the gentlemen of the Right complain of. In fact, during the course of American history, most government intervention has either been demanded by big business— *e.g.* the tariff, the rail and shipping subsidies, the imperialist posture, the highways—or it has been obligated by excesses of big business that had to be countervailed—*e.g.* the regulatory agencies, pure food and drug acts, Social Security, the Wagner act. But the present interventions—*e.g.* Urban Renewal or the education acts—are unique in that by the same expansive policy they favor big business and are also Liberal responses to the excesses of big business. There is nothing to limit or oppose them. (Perhaps the embattled farmers of West Greenwich Village.) By the same token, it is no longer possible to distinguish government and big business.

Take twenty random items, each of which in its place might be useful and some of which are indispensable. Installment buying, the National Science Foundation, fringe benefits, government home financing, arbitration, area development, support for high culture, research in new drugs, tax reform, urban transit systems, high schools for the gifted, remedial reading, applied social-psychology, two billion in contracted research in the universities, shopping centers, sponsored TV, job retraining, the campaign against dropouts, slum clearance, aid to underdeveloped countries. Weld these together in the heat of forced producing and forced consuming and suddenly they constitute, as I have said, one social machine running for its own sake. There is no longer any pluralism or countervailing power. To be a Liberal means to buy the whole package. To be a "conservative" and balk on this or that item means to be self-contradictory and confused. The only way of getting out of the trap, so that real choices can be made, is to change the real constitution, the proportion of the kinds of enterprise.

8

The immediate purpose of a mixed system at present
is to relax this interlocking, which has become critical
for democracy. Instead of the frantic effort to make
everything work at once and at an increased tempo, it
is wiser to give more chance to different auspices and
methods of organization to do what they can do best
and cheapest. Useful services must not be neglected
because they are inappropriate to the dominant style,
and basic necessities must not depend on the smooth
working of a whole economy. And we must reopen
opportunities for people to work and live in ways that
suit them, otherwise engagement is impossible, and we
have universal anomie.

Expanding the GNP with an interlocked economy is
a kind of dream of a "pure" economist, aiming at a
mathematical maximum of transactions, no matter
what. The policy of a mixed system is political economy in a period of high productivity, aiming at security, authentic enterprise, inventiveness, and a quality
standard of living. It is the difference between the
affluence of a nation and the wealth of a nation. For
example with a mixed system, the GNP might sharply
fall and this be a good sign. For many operations in
cooperative enterprises avoid cash transactions; a quality standard of living is often less cluttered and often
costs less; the more skilled people are, the more they
do for themselves; it is simpler to open universal goods
for free appropriation. Such factors are anti-"economic," but they would at present be cultivated by a
political economist.

Nobody knows enough—and it would be a mistake
anyway—to make a blueprint dividing the functions of
society into mixed species and to say: "This should be
done by corporations, this by government bureaucra-

cies, this by cooperatives, this by families." Or "this should be automated, this should be made in small plants, this by domestic power tools, this by hand, and this isn't worth the trouble to make at all." Or "this should be calculated on the computer but this should be discussed face to face." Or "this should be durable, this should obsolesce, this should be faddish, and this should be evanescent." The positive relation of style and function can not be determined *a priori* but only by the attempt to perform the function. But we can nevertheless judge the negative: at least the structure of enterprise must not *prevent* the use of talents and methods that are obviously advantageous, it must not *debase* quality, it must not regiment persons and create anomie. I hope I have shown that there is such a study as appropriateness of organizational style. In spite of Jacques Ellul, there is a difference between politics and "technology."

9

To end this chapter, let me comment on three topics important in our present situation: automation, the public sector, and the standard of living.

Automation and computer technology have great moral advantages. Obviously they go a long further step in freeing a mass of people from jobs from which they were alienated anyway, repetitive manual operations and routine clerical work. (It is said that many of the lower-grade jobs in automatic plants are unnatural in pace and too lonely, but these things can be accommodated.) More significant in the long run, I think, is that automation and computing will replace many tribes of "middle management," the junior executives and market calculators who are the main body of W. H. Whyte's Organization Men. These have been, humanly speaking, the group worst off in modern corporations.

Unlike top-management, they have not had the satisfactions of planning and running the show, yet they
have not had the union protection and really shorter
hours of the semi-skilled. They suffer the most emotional anxiety in maintaining status. (I suspect that
these are the types who, in college, are most eager, and
angry, to talk about decentralization.) Finally, this
technology requires a large increase in the number of
the highly trained and ingenious, as designers and programmers; and these, as they come to recognize themselves as indispensable, should be an interesting group
in society, very unlike Organization Men.

But the bother with this technology is that, in our
present mental climate, there is an epidemic disposition
to apply it everywhere, relevant or not. It will crack
oil at the right temperatures and pick out the right
nuts and bolts. It will diagnose syndromes, do legal
clerking, and compose minuets. It hires and grades and
admits to college. It does political and psychological
research (often without prior analysis; it is very fashionable to run twenty-three variables) and it abstracts
scientific articles. As we have seen, it will drive your
car down the highway for you. The issue is not, however, whether or not it can do some of these things
well; that remains to be seen, it is ongoing. The issue is
that factors which cannot, or cannot yet, be put on
tapes are simply dropped out of sight, though they
may be the essence. And conversely, theories are
"proved" and action is taken by stacks of processed
information that is quite irrelevant. Also, since personnel are not closely engaged with their functions and a
specious performance is as good as a real one, if an administrator thinks that he can save money by automat-
ing, he will surely automate and proudly bring his enterprise up to date. To put it bluntly, there could not
be a worse time in history or a worse place than Amer-

ica for automation and computing to come to flower.

Let me speculate about an appropriate pattern of use of automation. In principle, when the standard product of an automatic process (where the chief cost is the original capital) is excellent or quite good enough for universal use, it is rational to maximize the production to cut the price to the bone, and to treat the whole enterprise as a regulated monopoly. What is the sense of duplicating expensive tools in order to compete by minor variations? That is, *automatic production does not seem to be a plausible field for capitalist competition. But there might well be competition in designing improved pilot models for periodic re-tooling;* and then the competing teams should be as independent and decentralized as possible, in order to multiply points of view and progress rapidly.

Consider expensive commodities like automobiles or TV equipment. Would not the majority of people be happier with one standard model that was *very* cheap, and that was radically improved every time we vote for President? (Meanwhile we could *vote* on the next improvements.) This has been, of course, the European tradition grounded in established class differences: to have one good rather cheap model, and other expensive very special models. In America we have chosen a different pattern: there is no cheap model at all, and no really deluxe model either except for trimmings. With automation, however, the difference in cost could become so great, the good standard model could be so very cheap, that only the European pattern makes sense. What we have in America is a complex system of semi-competition with several-times-duplicated capital, charging a high fixed price for rather trivial variety. But automatic production calls for uniformity at a very cheap price, with freedom radically to improve the model.

On the other hand, in the functions of life where account must be taken of individual differences, personal contact, spontaneity, insight, synoptic view of the whole—thus, in education, social work, community planning, psychiatry, personal service, politics, arts, or fundamental research—it is probably best to *expunge entirely* the standardizing and logistic approach. One must be wary even of dumb machines, even used as auxiliaries. It is amazing how much damage one innocent business machine in the office can do to a school, a neighborhood development, a hospital, or a publisher. In such functions, to have style, to be relevant, it is useful to do the arithmetic on your fingers and make up the alphabet.

10

The achievement of useful public goods or even necessities, that everybody is "for," is persistently hampered by being part of the interlocking system. The enterprises are non-commercial, yet they are always tied up in elaborate packages and justified by extrinsic considerations. Instead of something being done because it should be done, it becomes a means of pump-priming investment, of reducing unemployment, of policing, of training for the economy, of improving our image abroad, or of making money for promoters and bolstering an urban political machine. And in this context it becomes so expensive that it indeed needs extrinsic justification. This is old-fashioned pork-barreling become statesmanlike.

Climactic, of course, is the formation of a military or monkish "helper" class—as in the War on Poverty or the expansion of something called "Education"— where a chief aim of the programs is to reduce the unemployment of the professional middle class. This is a worthy cause, but not the most direct way of balancing an unbalanced economy.

The style was developed mainly during the New Deal. Nevertheless, in that time of crisis, the New Deal included also a strong admixture of direct and essentially decentralized approaches; just as the turbulent labor movement of the period often had a beautiful local spontaneity. (It was after the resumption of "normalcy" that both government and labor became exclusively centralist.) We have already noticed the countervailing decentralism of the Farm Security Administration and the TVA. The WPA, the arts projects in the PWA, and the CCC were fairly direct methods of relieving unemployment. In the WPA and the arts projects, skilled people who needed employment were given the means and opportunity to use their skills for the public advantage, period. There was very little fuss about clearance, supervision, or administration, and an enormous amount of competent work was done dirt-cheap. (At its peak, the WPA theater comprised nearly sixteen thousand theater people at an average of $20 a week, and it played to fifteen million people.) In the CCC, professionals thought up public projects that unemployed youth could do, and the evidence is that where the projects were well conceived, the educational experience was worthwhile and the products have proved economically valuable far beyond their cost.

But the converse approach would be even more direct: to start with things that need doing and to find available skill and labor willing to do them. This procedure is rational and does not require emergencies. Consider a concrete case. There is a public good, improving the appearance of a small town or an urban neighborhood, that nobody is going to care for because there is no money in it and it is not "critical." There is also plenty of appropriate labor, a vast number of adolescents whose time is being wasted in so-called schools and who would gladly paint and repair a neighborhood if the school money were given to them. (It costs more than $1,100 a year to keep a youth in a New York blackboard jungle.) My guess is that there is many a public enterprise, including some highly intellectual and professional ones, that would cost next to nothing, if it could be kept independent of the interlocking economy, the labor unions, the politicians, and professional-personnel. This was, incidentally, the theory of the Domestic Peace Corps, but it fell into the hands of the Department of Justice, professional-personnel, the public school system, and (some say) politicians; these managed both to complicate the intention and to eat up the budget.

It is characteristic of an affluent society with high-level planning and highly complex organization that it cannot *afford* to paint a row of houses, keep its streams unpolluted, provide counsel in court for the poor, put out a cheap complete edition of American classical authors, support repertory theater and opera, have competing newspapers in large towns, etc., etc.

On the other hand, the "public sector" of the economists—*e.g.* Galbraith or Keyserling, or even men strongly oriented to human values like Mike Harrington or the authors of the *Triple Revolution*—tends to be unexamined in its auspices and consequences, except for the capacity to produce employment. In all lists of pump-priming proposals in the public sector, the three chief items are Housing, Schools, Highways. There is indeed a need for new housing, but the public methods of housing so far employed, *e.g.* Urban Renewal or public mortgaging, have largely increased dislocation, suburbanization, segregation, and anomie. Under the present auspices, as I have argued in *Compulsory Mis-Education,* we ought at present to have less schooling rather than more; the schools are the wrong way to spend money on the education of the young; they are brainwashing and regimenting. And the highway policy is an unmitigated disaster. The current revival of interest in more balanced transit is more promising; yet, again, the balance is not discussed in the functional context of regional and neighborhood planning and trying to *diminish* the need for commutation altogether; the "better" the transit, considered in isolation, the more the suburbanization and conurbation.

It is a painful thought: spending on the unexamined "public sector," with irrelevant purposes and centralized auspices, can be even worse than the present shameful neglect.

The War on Poverty, too, is strangely mesmerized by the central economic system. For instance, in Appalachia a furniture factory was subsidized for $1,800,-000 which, before it failed, gave employment for less than three years to one hundred workmen, at $1.25 an hour; would it not have been more imaginative to give each man $18,000? Again, the Job Corps camps will spend upward of $2,700 a year on each youth, excluding capital costs, to teach him remedial reading and a marketable skill that may be outmoded by the time he learns it. He cannot be simply paid as an apprentice.

11

Another characteristic of an affluent society, and a direct corollary of the interlocked system, is that it is hard to be decently poor, whether by choice or because one is too busy to make money. A person is either in the system or entirely marginal, on the verge of being out-caste. The 300-per-cent or more inflation caused by overhead, status salaries, union wages, taxes and tax evasion, etc., results in prices all along the line that a person cannot afford unless he adopts the same manners and makes the same kind of money. Jobs that are entirely authentic because of their simplicity, like dishwasher, hospital orderly, or migrant farm-worker, are paid strictly according to the Iron Law of Wages, slightly less than subsistence. Thus "voluntary poverty," as in the ideology of the Beats or the *Catholic Worker*, becomes submission to unprotected exploitation.

Unfortunately, just the people most deeply engaged in their work are likely to be at the worst disadvantage. For example, to preserve the spirit of justice, the most important clients of a lawyer are those charged with run-of-the-mill crimes and usually too poor to raise bail, but a lawyer cannot afford to keep taking such cases. The most important medical practice is probably preventive medicine by family visits, but all the money is in specialization and office visits. In the past, fine artists have tended to gravitate to decent poverty and have managed to live well; but at present it is expensive to drive even an old car, it is impossible to find cheap loft space and eat well cheaply, there is no way of showing without catering to the dealers. People in radical politics or in the Friends' kind of social work have the same problem. And the same holds for people who have no specially important work but who would like to live in their own way, usefully to themselves and others, and who do not need expensive commodities to fill their time or show off. In our society, as J. K. Galbraith has pointed out, just those who could make good use of their leisure, rarely have the leisure to do it, whereas the unemployed are usually without inner resources.

This difficulty of decent poverty for the intellectuals is a more crucial matter than perhaps seems. We have seen that managers and the best professional-personnel are desperately overworked and have little time for citizenship or the community. Yet the complicated conditions of urbanism and massification, rife with anomie and brainwashing, desperately need a big leavening of people who are disinterested, attentive, secure, and initiating. Where are they to come from? Meantime, one of the most dangerous and distressing aspects of contemporary America is the emergence of an immense academic, professional, and intellectual class that is entirely organized into the dominant system; and, conversely, the rapid disappearance of the independent, often dissenting but respectable, academics, professionals, and intellectuals who are the guardians of civilization. The economy tends to polarize the intellectuals into either bureaucrats or beatniks. In education, correspondingly, we have the dilemma that more and more of the young are compelled into the schools for longer years, but fewer adults who know something are willing to teach rather than pursue more profitable careers.

The involuntary poor, those who would be happy to enter the inflated economy but are "underprivileged," are entirely trapped. They do not know how to make do, do not know the ropes, have no connections. They are cheated in housing and installment buying, are extraordinarily ignorant as consumers, are unskilled in doing for themselves. Their difficult poverty degenerates to permanent squalor and degradation. Four thousand dollars is usually estimated as the minimum decent income for a small urban family; but, whereas independent, educated people with connections can manage without degradation on maybe as little as half of this, the stupefied hard-core poor probably need even more than $4,000 to get them on their feet. Typically, if things become too wretched, experienced and independent people make a move, perhaps out of the city altogether; but stupefied people never have choices open to them. Independent poor people who know the ropes are prudent about choosing cheap and safe vices, staying out of expensive trouble, entertaining themselves at little cost. But the underprivileged poor are like driven sheep; just to live on from day to day in their misery, they get caught in expensive and dangerous vices and need the commodities and entertainment that are advertised on TV. Inevitably an increasing number are reduced to being clients of public agencies, hospitals, and jails. This rouses the rage of the Conservatives and the alarm of the Liberals, but neither group thinks of simplifying the unviable conditions of life that make it impossible for simple or disadvantaged people to cope. Rather, as mental illness increases, their therapeutic wisdom is to complicate life still further by expanding the GNP, requiring more diplomas, and getting more people off the farms.

CHAPTER VII

Cyclical Swing

1

In an historical view, one can see cyclical swings from decentralized to centralized and overcentralized and back. Swings are in the nature of the case, since there are always forces in both directions. Concentrating power and rationalizing administration and production weld peoples into a centralized system by coercion or because there are real efficiencies and advantages. But a central authority can become too willful or taxes too high; lines of communication become too long or the distribution of imperial products too costly. Then people rebel, build their own factories, and try to rationalize production according to their own local customs, and they make shift decentrally because there are real efficiencies and advantages.

Especially when there is a radically new opportunity, there is a decentralizing trend, for the central style is old-fashioned with respect to it, and the persons who understand it and are good at it want to cut loose and proceed on their own. This can go as far as revolution. But the revolution, according to the modern theory, succumbs to the "bureaucratization of the prophetic" or the "iron law of oligarchy." (Not accidentally, the theorists of our century are good at proving that revolutions cannot "really" succeed.) On the other hand, there are routinized systems of prestigious authority, like the Catholic Church, where plenty of life goes on as if the central authority did not exist. Also, small "neutral" countries carry on peaceably for generations, once they have gotten over trying to be Powers.

All this is familiar. But formal historians usually concentrate on the centralizing swing, for that is where the history is: the concentration of power and growth of grandeur are more likely to have names and official chronicles. Small neutral nations are neglected in history books, though their citizens are adequately represented in the history of civilization. And historians would almost never use the word "decentralizing" to describe an important counter-movement. If their judgment of the decentralization is negative, they call it "decline and fall"; if it is positive, they call it "liberation from the old regime." In either case they hurry on to recover from the dark ages or to erect the new regime out of the disorder. Or sometimes millions of persons suddenly drop out of world history, for things have ceased to "happen" with them.

I am reminded of the indignant question of Coleridge when an economist declared that a village that did not take part in the national trade was of no importance. "What, sir, are five hundred Christian souls of no importance?"

To anarchist writers, it seems as if academic and Marxist writers are always describing the failure of a revolution, namely the new regime, when they think they are describing a revolution. Wolin calls his book on the Russian Revolution *The Unknown Revolution* the "real" revolution, he says, was effected by peasants, guerrillas, and mutinous sailors; it was systematically crushed by both foreign imperialists and Bolshevists. The same has been said of the Spanish Civil War; a revolution was being made by peasants and miners, but it was stopped by liberals, communists, and fascists. In writing on the French Revolution, Kropotkin wants to tell how provincial towns managed to organize society when freed from the incubus of Paris. I myself am evidently more interested in the politics of the Articles of Confederation than of the Constitution.

2

The escape of the serfs from the feudal domains to the growing towns of the eleventh and twelfth centuries—"town air makes free"—is best regarded as a great swing to decentralization. The new opportunity was the revival of trade, and the fugitives became craftsmen. In the framework of a fairly uniform law and a common religion, the town societies managed to organize themselves locally in multitudes of voluntary craft and professional associations, and they organized themselves across the languages of Europe in formal and informal federations of trade and science. In his history of the commune of Florence, Machiavelli calls this decentral town constitution of the Middle Ages the highest achievement of human politics, more glorious than the simplicity of early Rome. (So the author of *The Prince!* Karl Marx, similarly, said that the highest achievement of humanity had so far been the Elizabethan yeomanry!)

In fact, these towns—associations of associations, some of which were hierarchical, some democratic—invented modern technology, founded the modern uni-

versity, hit on modern corporate law, and by and large
created modern civilization.

This is the bread and butter of social and cultural
historians. Yet most political historians, in describing
this period, *prospectively* lay their emphasis on the
feudal wars and the emergence of the national sovereigns who took the towns over, destroyed their free-
doms, standardized and took the life out of the culture,
destroyed the inter-language community, emasculated
the universities and bureaucratized the guilds, nationalized the religion, and turned centers of civilization into
capital headquarters for the old business of tax collecting, policing, and warring on a grander scale.

3

In the seventeenth and eighteenth centuries, the development of the Enlightenment and the Industrial
Revolution was a swing to decentralization. This time,
the voluntary associations were friend-groups, partnerships, and companies of individuals rather than
corporate bodies. They banded together to enterprise
in their own way, free of royal monopolies, mercentil-
ist regulations, and the ossified relics of guilds, universities, and feudalism. Scientists and scholars tended
to go it alone, by correspondence, and in independent
academies. Stockholders in joint-stock companies were
vigilant of management. And these groups federated
across national boundaries for trade, science, technical
innovation, and political action. Out of it came political economy and modern social theory, the first colonial revolutions, the Bill of Rights, the limitation of
absolute power, the critical philosophy, the theory of
perpetual peace—in brief, everything that we now
think of as our best.

Yet the emphasis of both social and political historians is again, prospective: they talk about cash eco-

nomics and absentee ownership, enclosure, national aggrandizement and imperialism, the proletarianization of labor, all of which were antithetic to the Enlightenment, political economy, and the French Revolution. Typical is the astonishing one-sided stress on Calvinism and divisive individualism in explaining seventeenth- and eighteenth-century rationalism ("rationalization"), as if the age had not also been mad for mathematics and inventions, and yearning for natural man, equality, and fraternity, which were spontaneous factors in rationalizing. The Enlightenment version of the neoclassic style is highly standard and communicable, but it is not at all centralist; on the contrary, it was again a common framework in which intellectual groups could satirize and go their own way.

Sometimes the prospective reference is not even one-sided but simply inaccurate. For instance, a scholarly dedication and energy are attributed to the centralized German universities after the unification, which had really developed during a brilliant hundred years before, in autonomous academies and city-state universities, and which indeed the centralized universities succeeded in transforming into pedantry and chauvinistic *Kultur*.

4

Our modern centralization is unique in that it pervades so many details of life, like an intensely ritualistic religion or a garrison state (it has aspects of both). So I have singled out the *style* of it, rather than protesting that it impedes some particular liberty, like free trade or free speech, or that it involves excessive public and corporation taxation. But recently every writer has criticized it in particular—*The Tastemakers, The Insolent Chariots, The Lonely Crowd, The Organization Man, The Hidden Persuaders, The Tyranny of*

Testing, Mass Leisure, The Exurbanites, Compulsory Mis-Education, The Status Seekers, The Affluent Society, Growing Up Absurd, The Paper Economy, Silent Spring, The Child Worshipers, The Death and Life of Great American Cities, The American Way of Death—all these books, good or bad, are about the same thing: the irrelevance and destructiveness of a system running for its own sake and sometimes running wild.

Unfortunately, a corollary of dealing with a pervasive style is that it is hard to think not in the style. Voltaire could simply say *Ecrasez l'Infame* because he could conceive of simply doing without *l'Infame*. For us, it is only after we have gotten out of the interlocking system that we will be able to see how much of it was unnecessary.

Certainly the surplus productivity requires a basic overhauling of economic concepts. Accumulated wealth and new technology are now so productive and plastic that they can no longer plausibly be managed on classical economic principles of allocating scarce human and material resources. But the dominant system can only repeat its routine motives and routine method—reinvesting, expanding the Gross National Product. And with this goes the grotesque disproportion between the "hard" money that many unfortunate people work for and relievers starve on, and the giveaway money of fringe benefits, expense accounts, foundation grants, inflated salaries, and other tax dodges. In these circumstances, political economy and moral economics are impossible.

So psychologists, sociologists, and moral philosophers are busy re-analyzing basic economic concepts like "work," "unemployment," "property," "standard of living," "incentive," "security," etc. And they seem to end up by proposing everything on land or sea or in

the air, from Dr. Skinner's universal operant conditioning to Dr. Leary's universal use of psychedelic
drugs—both at Harvard. In my opinion, more significant than the content of these philosophies are two
characteristics of their form: in them, the world seems
open again to choice, we can choose how to live; yet
they are curiously unpragmatic and lacking in news
with regard to daily life and common mores. That is,
arbitrary choice is taken seriously in the most far-out
proposals, just when it is entirely vanishing in simpler
matters like schoolgoing, looking for a job, working at
a job, the layout of streets, housing, shopping, being
informed, politics. Just so, Donald Michael, in *The
Next Generation,* predicts that our society will continue as at present, only more interlocked and more abstract, but there will be plenty of asylums for the sensitive and intelligent to express themselves, like Indians
on a reservation.

Since I am conservative by disposition, I am not
quite so ready to remake human nature (even according to my own blueprint), nor to scuttle the culture of
the Western world. In my opinion, precisely the simpler matters—housing, shopping, being informed, and
making a living—are the most important matters, and I
set a high value on democratic initiative and deciding.
Thus, if we have choices, I am led to speak for decentralizing—"where it is feasible." This modest philosophy may be utopian, but it *is* pragmatic.

5

The idea of building-in decentralization is full of
dilemmas, if not contradictions. Let me conclude this
little book by discussing some of the dilemmas and
some of the opportunities.

First, in community development. There is a reali-
zation, that has penetrated even government agencies,

that urban anomie and the hopelessness of rural areas
that have lost their economies cannot be manipulated
away by simply importing social and medical services,
or even money. Somehow the remedies do not add up
to the whole that has been lost. Delinquency and ad-
diction do not succumb to clinics any more than to
policing and reformatories; retraining gets few takers;
and my guess is that we shall find that dropout and
youth unemployment are not materially helped by
"better" schools. Instead, people become further dependent on precisely the remedial services.

The new wisdom is that the neighborhood or depressed area must "participate" in its own reconstruction. So urban extension agents, youth workers, and
community developers are commissioned to help
groups to help themselves. But what is "administered
participation"?—the phrase is from a fine study of the
dilemma by Martin Cohnstaedt. The techniques are
decentral: to call local meetings and charter local
boards; to go along with the youth ideology in gang or
high school; to work side by side with the natives. But
the goals, alas, are from headquarters: to get tenants to
consent to relocation; to get kids to make less trouble
or do their lessons; and to get the natives to see that
Americans are good Joes. It is too early to judge, but I
doubt that this rather immoral pattern can work when
the chips are down. Certainly, Negroes have been ex-
pressing fierce resentment of liberals who know the
answers for them.

Not surprisingly, an effective means of temporary
community re-integration has been to help depressed
people just to vent their spite, for spite is the vitality of
the powerless. Protesting and circumventing arouse
spirit. And all the better if there are also tangible positive results, like bringing to court the short-measure
grocer, as in Woodlawn, or rent striking, as in Harlem.

But this kind of activity, too, does not add up. It blows off steam rather than creates a community.

The more sophisticated philosophy of community development is to have no "goal" at all, but to be a "catalyst." As William Biddle analyzes it, the professional who wants to help must morally commit himself to the community and offer what knowledge he has, but he must expect that any solution that emerges will be different from anything he expects. In one of Biddle's reports of work in a depressed area, there is a striking incident of the community suddenly *remembering* that long ago it used to thrive on a different economic base from the later industry that had moved out; having remembered it, people were able to return to it in a new and viable form. This sounds like excellent psychotherapy.

But finally, the best means of creating community is to delegate power. Participation means initiating, deciding, acting. If we mean to restore health—in psychotherapy, too—we must give back the power to function in the areas that are still vital. Consider an important current problem: There is bitter complaint of police brutality and venality in depressed urban neighborhoods, and as a remedy, the leaders of minority groups ask for civilian review boards; with typical liberalism, they add on a new level of administration, in which the neighborhood is "included" and has a voice. But surely a more direct remedy would be, as far as possible, to *give back* the administration and personnel of the police to the neighborhood itself. Then both the enforcement and the *interpretation* of the law would be in accordance with local public sentiment. The aim of police law is to keep the peace; it is not to enforce an impossible conformity on millions of people of all conditions. (As it is, graft is more relevant and less damaging than attempts at reform.)

So, in an earlier chapter, I suggested empowering the neighborhood school board, giving the neighborhood the power to plan its own redevelopment, and districting municipal functions so as to form a local City Hall. To put it bluntly, when a neighborhood can hire and fire, it might welcome outside professional help; and the professional can act rationally, instead of like a wet nurse or a psychiatrist.

In this context, there is an excellent use for the public underwriting of "advocates," as proposed by Edgar Cahn of the Office of Economic Opportunity. These are persons trained in law and administration who, when called on, can teach poor people the ropes and represent them if necessary. Thus, instead of being ruled by experts who know what is good for them, poor people—like rich people—can have available experts whom they can use. This must lead to new confidence.

6

Similar dilemmas occur in industry and business. It is now the fashion to try to make workers less alienated, more "belonging," and generally happier, by profit sharing, insurance benefits, recreation facilities, and the improvement of psychological conditions of work. The purpose of these devices is to prevent labor disputes and increase efficiency, and they somewhat work. But the evidence is that they do *not* create identity with the rational goals of the organization, but rather increase dependency on the organization. That is, the men are treated like children and they become childish.

(It seems to me that this is the significant interpretation of the "Hawthorne effect," that people respond to participating in the experiment, to being paid attention to, no matter what the content or ultimate purpose of the experiment. It is dismaying that adults on a job should be so infantile and so little able to further their own objective interests.)

Researching job attitudes, Frederick Herzberg of Western Reserve has developed a valuable psychiatric distinction between the health producing and the merely protective or hygienic. The health producing, says Herzberg, is inner-motivated, task-engaged, outgoing; it is, finally, that which enables a man to exercise power. The hygienic is that which avoids anxiety or emotional stress. A workman is happy on the job when the work is interesting, when he uses his capacities, when he can use initiative; he is "not unhappy" when conditions are pleasant, when he has security, when his dignity is not insulted.

Let us draw an obvious moral. Bosses and managers could far more directly improve the conditions of work if, instead of indulging in paternalism, they would cut out the unnecessary authoritarianism and time controlling that in fact make people dependent and spiritless. In any big office, for example, a good part of the day is spent by a good many people doing nothing and trying to look busy. In such an office it is a big deal and a subject of gratitude if, on a hot day, the boss dismisses people early. Isn't this childish? As adults, the workers have agreed to do a job for a wage; then why cannot they themselves tailor the schedule to the job, including doing work at home when that is just as efficient? Think of it, grown people phone in lying excuses about not coming in.

When a man applies at a plant and there are several open stations requiring equivalent skill, it would certainly be intelligent to let him try them and choose. If the attempt to make him "belong" were authentic, a workman would be encouraged to change his station and get to know various parts of the operation; that is, he would be treated like the boss's son. Instead, he has to compete and be well-behaved in order to be "promoted" to a higher bracket, as though he were still in grade school.

A good arrangement for treating men as responsible agents is the collective contract that I mentioned in Chapter I. The gang makes its own schedule and rules and hires and fires. Presumably the men in the gang know their own skills and interests better than a production manager does.

In automatic production, it is plausible, as I suggested in Chapter VI, that model changes and re-tooling might also best be devised by teams working decentrally. This would allow much fresher perspective. And it is all the more appropriate since in such production there must be a great increase of the highly skilled and ingenious, as designers and programmers, who also know more about the whole operation than formal management is likely to.

To be sure, all these suggestions involve, in one way or another, the possibility of workmen taking part in management, and this is the point at which American management balks, and American unions do not press. Yet it is hard to see why any of them would be less productively efficient or even necessarily diminish profits.

7

The American educational system is easier to decentralize, sweepingly, from bottom to top, since teaching and learning consist entirely in face-to-face and community relations, and the present overcentralization has no authentic functions at all. The schools are being used as universal baby-sitter and time-occupier, and as apprentice training for a few industries. But there are simpler, more enjoyable, and more efficient ways to perform these functions. (The other great present use of the schools, for the aggrandizement of school systems and universities, is better just forgotten.)

It is claimed by the National Science Foundation that since the new technology requires more specialized skills, the schools must generally be more tightly geared to centrally improved curricula. This argument is singularly wrong-headed. If a relatively few will work in that technology, it is senseless to waste the general time on specialist skills. It would be far more just and more efficient for the relevant industries to pay for and administer special training, rather than getting half-apprentices at the public and parents' expense. That is, at present we need *less* centralized schooling than we did.

Colleges, high schools, and primary schools could all usefully be cut down in size and run by their faculties and staff. The present framework of administration and outside social pressuring are merely distracting and wasteful. The whole extrinsic rigmarole of credits, prescribed syllabus, competitive grading, and promotion up the ladder is pedagogically destructive and should simply be scrapped. There is little evidence that a student learns anything of value if he has learned it merely to pass; and those who want to learn a subject at their own time and according to their own interest are interrupted by the schedule and misled by extrinsic motivation.

But more important, the concept that all "education" should be administered by school people is a delusion of overcentralization. It is impossible that long continuous years of sitting in schoolrooms is the appropriate means of educating most people to be useful to themselves and society. Yet we are now trying to keep 100 per cent in school till eighteen, and by 1970

50 per cent will be in colleges. Very many youngsters, including very many of the bright, are stupefied by the methods and language of the academic setting. Given the variety of conditions and talents, we should be exploring and experimenting many settings to educate, and pay as much attention as possible to individual differences and signs of choice.

The centralizing approach is to abstract from the functions of society, whatever they happen to be, and to put the abstractions in a school-box as the curriculum. The decentralist approach would be to turn directly to the functions of society that might be educated for, and to open in them opportunities for the young to take part. Academic learning is for the academically talented. We have just mentioned the responsibility of the corporations to provide schooling for their own apprentices, and also their workmen. (In this respect, by the way, the armed services are not a bad model, not only for teaching radar but also for teaching to read.) In a previous chapter, we mentioned using school money to help finance worthwhile activities that will otherwise be neglected, *e.g.* some public works, independent broadcasting and newspapers, little theaters; these provide educational opportunities and immensely broaden the range of choice. (See Appendix IV.) Also, it is reasonable to extend the idea of the GI Bill to the high schools: to give the school money directly to the student to pursue any course he chooses that is plausibly educational. This would have the advantage of multiplying experimental schools, sorely needed in our present monolithic system.

Another gross defect of the tightly interlocked continuous system is that it discourages leaving and re-entry, whereas these are in the essential nature of the educational process. There must be moratoria in growing up, and one must accumulate other experiences and scenes than doing lessons. Young people now come to college who are too young, who have never done or seen anything, and who are ineducable in university subjects. On the other hand, there are times when mature people need and want academic learning and could profit immensely by it; but they are stymied by the bureaucratic system of credits and diplomas irrelevant to their actual situation.

8

Decentralizing the interlocking communications is imperative, to make democracy possible. In Appendix VI, I suggest a general social policy and an expedient to multiply independent media.

But there is no doubt that writers and artists could do much more for themselves than they do, to countervail homogenization and brainwashing. The mass media cannot do without original and highly talented people; if even a few score of these would band together, they could importantly liberate editorial policy. (It seems to me that the same holds for the chief scientists of all countries, in forcing disarmament.) Just as the AAUP protects academic freedom by publicizing and boycotting, we could defend against wiping out and editing our tapes, against format that kills free expression, against rewriting that takes the life out of style, and against blacklisting. A barrage of exposure, satire, and orneriness would do the trick.

When I have made feeble efforts to awaken such concerted action, however, I have been appalled at the lack of community of art and letters in this country as contrasted with France or England. Intellectuals will combine to protest a particular abuse or censorship, but they seem unable to regard themselves as a uniquely responsible corporation, though we have constitutional powers. Of course, competitiveness and envy are strongly divisive among artists and writers, and many are chary about "joining" anything, whether for economic advantage or reasons of ideology. Yet we are unanimous about freedom of expression and autonomy of style, and we alone understand the problems. We could cooperate.

In the face of mass values in publishing, it is surprising that cooperative houses do not arise. A few disgruntled editors and a few well-known authors could make a go of it independently; they have the skills and the guaranteed sales. (The costs of publishing are about the same for small houses and big houses.) But well-known writers are economically satisfied where they are. They would need a new notion of their social function in order to want to publish their own way. The problem has been more acute for advance-guard writers or those who do not use the salable genres. Occasionally, a fairly big house—I shall name no names—has specialized in this new and non-commercial writing, but it is as with off-Broadway: the house is looking, prospectively, for "successes." (Typically, Beckett is rejected; then, when he has made a success, he is sought out.)

Smaller advance-guard publishers, like Jonathan Williams or Ferlinghetti, are more authentic, but cliquish and marginal. It seems to me that there could be a federation of such houses, that would increase promotion and put them all in a more powerful position. Certainly there should be federations of little magazines. The irregular and short-lived careers of little magazines destroy the chance for circulation to grow; a federation could guarantee that a subscriber will regularly receive something or other for his money. As I have pointed out, different little magazines of one tendency get their material from exactly the same pool of artists and writers anyway; a federation would express this continuity. There have been efforts to form such federations, but apparently no one has yet hit on the right formula; or, more likely, no one with a good head for business has yet put it to this good use.

9

Probably the most characteristic of all our dilemmas is the "problem of leisure," as it is called. It is feared, alternatively, that with the maturation of automatic and computer technology, either people won't *have* to work and will degenerate; or there won't be anything for them to work *at*, and they will be unhappy spending their time in trivial leisure activities. (Indeed, culturally, the prospect of a great nation playing golf and folk-dancing is dismaying.)

The fear of degeneracy is mentioned mostly by our Conservatives, and is of the same vintage as the argument that unemployment insurance and Social Security must lead to general goofing off and milking the public treasury. (Similarly, a hundred years ago it was solemnly argued that the general public could not be trusted to have open access to the shelves of libraries.) In fact, everywhere that a detailed checkup of cheating has been made, the cost of the checkup has been many times the amount saved on cheaters. The bother has been the other way: when hours of work are cut, there is too much moonlighting.

The other fear, of having nothing to do with oneself, is expressed rather by Liberals. It has substance, but the problem is an artifact. It is an expression of the same spirit of dependency that we have noticed in depressed neighborhoods and in business and industry. If people have not been rendered stupid and powerless, by schools and liberals among others, they will no doubt know what to do with themselves. Psychologically, boredom is not a deprivation, the want of something to do; it is a positive act of repressing what is attractive but forbidden, and *then* there is nothing interesting to do.

The remedy of thoughtful Liberals is also typical, that we must get rid of our lust for productive activity and for being functional. The Aristotelian notion that happiness consists in activity is now considered "Calvinistic"; rather, we must learn "how to have a good time" or "self-development" and "self-actualization." (Liberals do not go as far as the psychedelic drugs— the *soma* of *Brave New World*—but some of them toy with *satori*.) What a remarkable sign of a system running for its own sake!—they are willing to entertain these extraordinary changes in the character of people rather than thinking of altering the way we do things, organizationally, economically, or technologically.

The paradoxes of surplus are pathetic. We can buy an assortment of beautiful hand power tools: they are lusted for—the sale is tremendous; yet they are mostly put to only trivial uses—the users cannot repair them—they are for Christmas presents and they lie broken like Christmas toys. At present, with the splendid equipment, the cars, and TV, the conditions of small farming are rather paradisal; judged all around, it is probably the most attractive way of life now available in the United States; even economically, it can be combined in many ways with cottage industry and factory jobs to earn enough cash. Yet the heart and community have vanished out of it, and nine out of ten youth will leave it. It is simply never entertained as one possibility of diminishing urban overcrowding and squalor. Again, there is a fantastic amount of schooling; we are flooded with profound books, in paperback, that correctly analyze the conditions of society and are a guide to life. Yet in fact almost no one is a free agent able to use his wits and act on what he knows, so the education and reading have no point.

Return now to the proposal for a guaranteed decent income. As I have said, I agree with this, for nothing else is moral. If goods are available, they must not be withheld from need and use. And I predict that—*as applied to the United States*—people will soon grasp this, and we shall have the guaranteed income. Besides, the guaranteed income is probably far more economical than our present welfare procedures. It would cost less in money, effort, and suffering than our social-work and means-test methods of coping with poverty, unemployment, and much of delinquency and crime. (Curiously, this kind of arithmetic is what the public can never grasp.)

Nevertheless, it will be a pity if this important change in our conditions of life is, as urged by the economists, simply tied to the expanding Gross National Product, and is not used as an opportunity toward a more mixed and open system. The freedom from unwanted and alienated work, and from "unemployment," should be accompanied by the opportunity for wanted and engaged work. The problem of guaranteed income is not whether the income should be given, but how it should be given.

In the first place, guaranteed income could be used as an occasion for dividing the subsistence economy from the general market economy, and directly and independently producing the subsistence. (Let us assume that subsistence constitutes half of the "decent income.") The advantage of segregating the production and distribution of subsistence is to remove this crucial universal necessity from the fluctuations and pressures of the rest of the economy; thus, to take care of first things first and so make the whole both more flexible and more secure. When we wrote *Communitas* twenty years ago, my brother and I estimated that maximum mass production and free distribution of "minimum" (American standard) subsistence would require about one tenth of the labor force, each person working a forty-hour week one year in ten. I have no idea what the ratio would dwindle to with automation, but my guess is that to produce subsistence for society would be a job wanted by many more people than there would be places available.

Again, in the preceding chapter we spoke of neglected community services and improvements that an affluent society cannot afford, but that would willingly be performed by people happy to live in decent poverty if they could do the work they wanted. Such work also could be regarded as "working for" the guaranteed income. (This would perhaps satisfy the scruples of those who do not think that people, especially serious people, should get something for nothing.) But note that this kind of world is *not* the "public sector"—housing, schools, highways, transit—that the economists talk about. It would not exist in the same system of union labor, public appropriations, contracting, and promotion. It would be voluntary and often exempt from central administration. (*E.g.* a neighborhood improvement, like the playground of the Harlem Education Project described above, is entirely a local affair. But a concerted voluntary effort to clean up a river requires central administration.) It would be a use of the guaranteed income to make the country lovely and its "leisure" meaningful.

Further, the economic motives of a new generation would inevitably be profoundly influenced by the pluralism of educational opportunity described in the last section. If young people grew up accustomed to try out where they could be useful and engaged, very many would be immune from the plague of extrinsic rewards; they would have found vocations and would *know* what they wanted to do with themselves. This is a more interesting proposition than the "good time" or the "self-actualization" of the anti-Calvinists. (Other people, perhaps the majority, who would still find their chief excitement in the things that money can buy, might then work to get rich at least by choice and not because of anxiety.)

Finally, the necessary sharp distinction that we must ultimately make between those goods and services that are appropriately automatic and those from which automation and computing should be expunged, will re-open many occupations. Instead of the skimping that now occurs in employment for human service, whether waiting on table or teaching school or caring for the insane, we may come to see that people are useful after all. Even indispensable. A beneficent, though unintended, result of the mass production and economic centralization of two centuries may yet be to give us the freedom to understand what needless sacrifices we have made for that mass production and centralization.

10

Surplus productivity, however, exists—or could soon exist—only in technologically advanced parts of the world, the United States, Europe, Japan; the relative poverty, and sometimes absolute poverty, of many other regions is sharply increasing. Thus, a strong political and moral case can be made for continuing to expand our economy and pouring the products into overseas aid; that is, it is not yet time, in the One World, for a guaranteed income in the United States. (Needless to say, this is not the thinking of the worshipers of the GNP.)

In my opinion, there are important distinctions to be made:

1. It is immoral, and certainly politically unwise, not to try to wipe out disease, hunger, and drudgery wherever they exist in the world. Such an effort involves exporting a certain amount of consumers' goods, especially in emergencies, but mostly commuity development, expert advice, education, and a very limited kind of producers' goods, namely the technology of basic subsistence, where it is necessary and usable. Given health and some education and leisure, a people can "take off" into a higher standard at its own pace. This is implicitly the philosophy of the Friends, UNICEF, the Peace Corps, and other service organizations.

2. It is an entirely different matter, however, to try to export the high standard and elaborate capital of technologically advanced nations, a process that necessarily results in a total change of local mores, the disruption of communities, forced urbanization, political bondage, and often tribal wars. Plus fantastic waste and over-commitment to mistakes. Inevitably, the Western-trained elite of backward peoples desire this kind of foreign capitalization; but it is also the philosophy espoused both by well-intentioned Westerners like C. P. Snow and by capitalists who have equipment to sell (often outmoded).

3. By and large, the export of our own high standard is a form of neo-imperialism, and has invariably turned underdeveloped regions into battlegrounds of the Cold War between Great Powers. It makes it impossible, for instance, for the United Nations to neutralize a region so that it can come to its own peace and government. Nor does this new kind of wealth, if any survives, filter down to the mass of the people. On the contrary, they are often reduced to a degradation worse than their worst poverty.

4. On the other hand, in our own country, the peaceful disposition, free of the taint of profits and power, and the personal friendliness, willingness to serve, and adventurousness necessary for the intercourse of peoples and the creation of a really equal One World, depend, it seems to me, on resolving our frantic domestic hang-ups, quieting down, learning to work for community use and not for money and status. In the fairly short run, the mass of the poor peoples of the world will get more help from happy young Americans than from harried ones.

Ultimately, let me say in a sentence, the lesson of decentralizing is the formation of the world community on a basis of functional regions rather than national states.

11

These, then, are the considerations that I present to college students who want to talk about decentralization, urging them to make the empirical studies that I am incompetent to make. It seems to me that they are interested.

But now I have before me an essay by Professor Hofstadter of Columbia who says that young people are not interested in these things at all. (It is significant that authors have begun to discuss this subject one way or another!) He cites a 1949 article from *Fortune*: "The class of '49 wants to work for somebody else. . . . The emergent young man is not afraid of bigness; where his father of the twenties, fearful of anonymity, was repelled by hugeness in an organization, he is attracted." He refers to David Riesman on the ideals of the class of '55, who reported "not only a bland acceptance of the large corporation as a place in which to do one's life work, but a depressing complacency about the terms and reward. . . . The class of '55 took the bureaucratic career for granted."

In 1963 and '64, my experience is different. The background has changed in this decade. The class of '64 has gone through the frantic post-Sputnik speed-up and regimentation in its own schooling. I recall how the remarkable revolt of the Beats created a panicky rage in these middle-class boys when they were freshmen; at that time they wanted to talk only about the Beats. Since 1955, the anomie has gone further; there are now riots in the streets. There is a new word, Automation, and it has raised questions. The Negro revolution has developed, and that has raised questions. The class of '64 was excited by the election of John Kennedy (I never could find a definite reason why); but his Administration was just different enough from Eisenhower's to be frustrating, and to raise questions. Maybe the Cold War has lasted too long and some of the pacifist talk has gotten through. We have seen that even the Right reaction is not a return to Big Business but to a perverted Populism.

Most important, the inquirers of '49 and '55 did not present alternatives, because alternatives were unthinkable. Trapped, the young had no other choice. But since then, they have sat-in, freedom-rode, and jumped up and down with signs. Perhaps just grown beards. Respectable economists have been presenting outlandish proposals like guaranteed income. There has been a revival of "utopian thinking." And here I came, saying that the overcentralized system was not even always the most efficient.

During 1963-64 at San Francisco State College, Kay Boyle says, "I conducted an inquiry into the opinions of the students. The response was overwhelming, *i.e.*, not one was satisfied with the education he was receiving, the temper ranging from outrage over the wasted energies and years, to grieved rebuke to parents and other authorities who should have known how tragically our educational system has failed. Their blue-prints were precise, exciting, tough-lingoed, and done with passionate conviction . . . they wanted 'inde-pendence, initiative, honesty, earnestness, utility, re-spect for thorough scholarship.' " (*New York Times*, October 18, 1964.)

When the first thousand volunteers of the Peace Corps returned and were asked what they liked best about the experience, "The most common response is the same, whether you ask a development worker in Latin America, a teacher in Africa, or a farmer in Asia. 'The freedom and autonomy I enjoyed.' 'The oppor-tunities for self-expression and creativity in my assign-ment.' 'The responsibility I was given for my age.' " (David Pearson, Deputy Information Director of the Peace Corps.) If this is the value they have learned, they have their work cut out for them in the United States.

North Stratford, New Hampshire

APPENDIX I

"Getting Into Power"[*]

1

The spirited candidacy of Stuart Hughes for Senator
—like an actualization of Leo Szilard's courageous plan
to finance and organize a national party for peace—
makes it useful to review the ambiguities involved in
this kind of politics.

"War is the health of the State"—modern history
teaches no other lesson, whether we think of the weird
personal, fanatic, and dynastic wars of the sixteenth
and seventeenth centuries or the economic and geopo-
litical wars of recent generations. The sovereign national States have lived and grown by preparing for
war and waging war; and as the Powers have aggrandized themselves, they have become more crashingly
destructive. I do not mean that men have not used also
simpler social organizations, feudal, tribal, free city, in
order to kill one another *en masse*, but centralized sovereign power, radiating from baroque capitals, has

* *Liberation*, October 1962.

proved to be the ideal executive of murderous will. In our own nation at present, it would be impossible to describe the economy without regarding war-making as a crucial factor; the foreign relations of the United States are carried on entirely in terms of bellicose power blocs, and either to expand "influence" or to hang onto it; and to mention my own field where I can speak at first hand, our primary education and heavily State-subsidized higher education have become regimented to apprentice-training for war, more directly if less sickeningly than the psychological national regimentation endemic in French and German schooling. (The Russians go in for both the technological and psychological aspects.)

This solidifying of national sovereign bellicosity is at present all the more irrational, and of course all the more necessary if the sovereigns are to maintain themselves, since the cultural, technological, economic, and communications relations of the world are now overwhelmingly supra-national. (What a pity that, partly to combat colonialism and partly out of the emulative stupidity and cupidity of their Western-trained leaders, peoples of Africa and Asia are adopting the same fatal and outmoded style.)

The only possible pacifist conclusion from these facts is the anarchist one, to get rid of the sovereignties and to diminish, among people, the motivations of power and grandiosity. This means, regionally, to decentralize or centralize directly in terms of life functions, empirically examined. My own bias is to decentralize and localize wherever it is feasible, because this makes for alternatives and more vivid and intimate life. It multiplies initiative. And it is safer. On the basis of this weakening of the Powers, and of the substitution of function for power, it would be possible also to organize the world community, as by the functional agencies of the United Nations, UNICEF, WHO, somewhat UNESCO; and to provide *ad hoc* cooperation like the Geophysical Year, exploring space, or feeding the Chinese.

Rigidly applied, this logic would seem to make pacifist State politics absurd. It is not in the nature of sovereign power to decree itself out of existence. (Thus, it is absurd for picketers of the White House to petition Mr. Kennedy as the President, rather than to sermonize him as a man or lecture him as a boy.) Also, such politics confuses the basic issue, that *pacifism is necessarily revolutionary*. A moment's recollection of the defection of the French and German socialist deputies from their pacifism in 1914 will show that this confusion is not trivial. Nevertheless, the attitude of the General Strike for Peace* is as follows: in November we shall urge people actively and explicitly to refuse to vote, to strike against voting, except for candidates who are unambiguously committed to immediate action to relax the Cold War, for instance Stuart Hughes or Robert Kastenmeier. Our reasoning is that, in our increasingly monolithic society and economy, any anti-war activity is likely to exert a revolutionary influence willy-nilly. And secondly, as Professor Hughes himself has said, the machinery of an electoral compaign *can* be a powerful means of education, especially by compelling mention of what the mass media ordinarily refuse to mention. We wish to cooperate with pacifist activity of *every* kind, whether SANE, Quaker, Third Party politics, or Committee for Nonviolent Action, because although "objectively" we are in a revolutionary situation in that the powers-that-be are certainly bent on destroying themselves and everything else, nevertheless people do not take this se-

---

* Mike Harrington, a Socialist, has recently pointed out in the *New Leader* that the GSP "suffers from an anarchist tinge."

riously and there is an almost total lack of practical will to make the necessary reorganization of society. To say it grimly, unlike 1914, people do not even have political representatives to betray them.

Personally, what I enjoy about Professor Hughes's campaign is that often, when the students were out getting signatures to put him on the ballot, people would say, "Do you mean he is *neither* a Democrat *nor* a Republican? Then give me the pen!" (It is said, by people from Massachusetts, that this response is peculiarly appropriate to the ordinary local politics of Massachusetts; but I take this as local boasting.) In the deadly routine that the Americans have sunk into, the mere possibility of an *alternative* is a glorious thing. Especially if there is the framework of a permanent organization. Also such a campaign must be a remarkable experience for Hughes himself, to confront many people who do not at all have the same assumptions. And it gives some concrete activity to his phalanx, the New England professors of the Council of Correspondence. The students of Brandeis, Harvard, etc., are also busy with it; but on them this *kind* of political involvement might be, in my opinion, more ambiguous, and that is why I am writing this essay.

2

For let me turn to an issue much deeper and more fateful for pacifism than these questions of strategy and tactics. This is the assumption, now appallingly unanimous among the ordinary electorate, professional politicians, most radicals, and even political scientists who should know better, that politics is essentially a matter of "getting into power," and then "deciding," directing, controlling, coercing, the activities of society. The model seems to be taken from corporations with top-management, and there is something prestig-

ious about being a "decision-maker." (Even C. Wright
Mills was mesmerized by this image; but, as I tried to
show recently in *Commentary*, in such a setup less and
less of human value is really decided by any responsible person, though plenty of disvalue is ground out by
the setup itself.) It is taken for granted that a man
wants "power" of this kind, and it is quite acceptable
for people like Joseph Kennedy and his sons to work
toward it, even though this is directly contrary to the
political ideal that the office and its duties seek the man
rather than the man the office. It is axiomatic that a
Party's primary purpose is to get into power, although
this was not the original idea of "factions," in Madison's sense, which were functional though divisive interest groups. More dangerously still, it is taken for
granted that a nation wants to be a Great Power, and
maintain itself so at any cost, even though this may be
disadvantageous to its culture and most of its citizens.*

And following the popular Leviathan like a jolly-
boat, the political-sociologists devote their researches
to the analysis and simulation of power struggles, as if
this were their only possible subject; and as advisers,
they take part in the power struggles, rather than helping to solve problems. Unfortunately, the thinking of
Hughes and Szilard seems to share some of this assumption about the paramountcy of "getting into
power"—just as David Riesman is always hounding
people who are in "power." And, frankly, when I
question such a universal consensus, I wonder if I am

* Recently Robert Frost, who has been losing his horse-sense
since becoming the friend of the President, told the Russians
in Moscow that a nation must be "great . . . in order to protect the language, the poetry." Yet in this century a majority of
the greatest writers of English have been Irish, *e.g.* Yeats, Synge,
Joyce, Shaw. So Rilke and Kafka were Czech and wrote, na-
tively, German. As the Jews have long known, it is best to
share in a world language and culture and to be free of the
prejudices, hypocrisy, and foolishness of Great Powers.

on the right planet. Nevertheless, these persons are deluded. They are taking a base and impractical, and indeed neurotic, state of affairs as if it were right and inevitable. The state of affairs is impractical because, finally, no good can come of it; though of course, since it *is* the state of affairs, it must be transiently coped with and changed. Unless we remember much more clearly than we seem to, what this "power" is, our behavior in the madhouse cannot be prudent and therapeutic. So with chagrin I find myself forced to review elementary political theory and history.

Living functions, biological, psychosociological, or social, have very little to do with abstract, preconceived "power" that manages and coerces from outside the specific functions themselves. Indeed, it is a commonplace that abstract power—in the form of "will power," "training," "discipline," "bureaucracy," "reform schooling," "scientific management," etc.— uniformly *thwarts* normal functioning and debases the persons involved. (It has a natural use, in emergencies, when not high-grade but minimal low-grade behavior is required.) Normal activities do not need extrinsic motivations, they have their own intrinsic energies and ends-in-view; and decisions are continually made by the ongoing functions themselves, adjusting to the environment and one another.

We may then define the subject of normal politics. It is the constitutional relations of functional interests and interest groups in the community in which they transact. This is the bread and butter of ancient political theory and obviously has nothing to do with sovereignty or even power—for the ancients the existence of Power implies unconstitutionality, tyranny. But even modern authors who move in a theory of "sovereignty," like Spinoza, Locke, Adam Smith, Jefferson, or Madison, understand that the commonwealth is strongest when the functional interests can seek their own level and there is the weakest exercise of "power." For instance, Spinoza tries to play power like a fish, Jefferson to de-energize it, Madison to balance it out, Smith to make it an umpire.

Let us now quickly sketch the meaning of the recent transcendent importance of "power" and "getting into power," as if otherwise communities could not function.

First, and least important, there is the innocuous, non-violent, and rather natural development of a kind of abstract power in an indigenous (non-invaded) society. The functions of civilization include production, trade and travel, the bringing up of the young in the mores; also subtle but essential polarities like experimentation and stability; also irrational and superstitious fantasies like exacting revenge for crime and protecting the taboos. Different interests in the whole will continually conflict, as individuals or as interest groups; yet, since all require the commonwealth, there is also a strong functional interest in adjudication and peace, in harmonizing social invention or at least compromise. It is plausible that in the interests of armistice and adjudication, there should arise a kind of abstract institution above the conflicts, to settle them or to obviate them by plans and laws; this would certainly be Power. (This derivation is plausible but I doubt that it is historical, for in fact it is just this kind of thing that lively primitive communities accomplish by quick intuition, tone of voice, exchange of a glance, and suddenly there is unanimity, to the anthropologist's astonishment.) Much more likely, and we know historically, abstract power is invented in simple societies in emergencies of danger, of enemy attack or divine wrath. But such "dictatorship" is *ad hoc* and surprisingly lapses. Surprisingly, considering that power corrupts; yet it makes psychological sense, for emergency is a negative function, to meet a threat to the preconditions of the interesting functions of life; once the danger is past, the "power" has no energy of function, no foreground interest, to maintain it. To give a very late example: it seemed remarkable to the Europeans, but not to the Americans, that Washington, like Cincinnatus, went home to his farm; and even the Continental Congress languished. There were no conditions for "power."

(Indeed—and this is why I have chosen the example—in the last decades of the eighteenth century, in many respects the Americans lived in a kind of peaceful community anarchy, spiced by mutinies that were hardly punished. The Constitution, as Richard Lee pointed out, was foisted on them by trickery, the work of very special interest groups; it would have been quite sufficient simply to amend the Articles.)

Altogether different from this idyl is the universal history of most of the world, civilized or barbarian. Everywhere is invasion, conquest, and domination, involving for the victors the necessity to keep and exercise power, and for the others the necessity to strive for power, in order to escape suffering and exploitation. This too is entirely functional. The conqueror is originally a pirate; he and his band do not share in the commonwealth, they have interests apart from the community preyed on. Subsequently, however, piracy becomes government, the process of getting people to perform by extrinsic motivations, of penalty and blackmail, and later bribery and training. But it is only the semblance of a commonwealth, for activity is not voluntary. Necessarily, such directed and extrinsically motivated performance is not so strong, efficient, spontaneous, inventive, well-structured, or lovely as the normal functioning of a free community of interests.

Very soon society becomes lifeless. The means of community action, initiative, decision, have been preempted by the powerful. But the slaveholders, exploiters, and governors share in that same society and are themselves vitiated. Yet they never learn to get down off the people's back and relinquish their power. So some are holding on to an increasingly empty power; others are striving to achieve it; and most are sunk in resignation. Inevitably, as people become stupider and more careless, administration increases in size and power; and conversely. By and large, the cultures that we study in the melancholy pages of history are pathetic mixtures, with the ingredients often still discernible: There is a certain amount of normal function surviving or reviving—bread is baked, arts and sciences are pursued by a few, etc.; mostly we see the abortions of lively social functioning saddled, exploited, prevented, perverted, drained dry, paternalized by an imposed system of power and management that preempts the means and makes decisions *ab extra*. And the damnable thing is that, of course, everybody believes that except in this pattern nothing could possibly be accomplished: if there were no marriage license and no tax, none could properly mate and no children be born and raised; if there were no tolls there would be no bridges; if there were no university charters, there would be no higher learning;* if there were no usury and no Iron Law of Wages, there would be no capital; if there were no markup of drug prices, there would be no scientific research. Once a society has this style of thought, that every activity requires licensing, underwriting, deciding by abstract power, it becomes inevitably desirable for an ambitious man to seek

---

* In *The Community of Scholars*, an anarchist critique of the colleges, I try to show how certain centers of learning were doing beautifully before they officially "existed" at all.

power and for a vigorous nation to try to be a Great Power. The more some have the power drive, the more it seems to be necessary to the others to compete, or submit, just in order to survive. (And importantly they are right.) Many are ruthless and most live in fear.

Even so, this is not the final development of the belief in "power." For that occurs when to get into power, to be prestigious and in a position to make decisions, is taken to be the social good itself, apart from any functions that it is thought to make possible. The pattern of dominance-and-submission has then been internalized and, by its clinch, fills up the whole of experience. If a man is not continually proving his potency, his mastery of others and of himself, he becomes prey to a panic of being defeated and victimized. Every vital function must therefore be used as a means of proving or it is felt as a symptom of weakness. Simply to enjoy, produce, learn, give or take, love or be angry (rather than cool), is to be vulnerable. This is different, and has different consequences, from the previous merely external domination and submission. A people that has life but thwarted functions will rebel when it can, against feudal dues, clogs to trade, suppression of thought and speech, taxation without representation, insulting privilege, the Iron Law of Wages, colonialism. But our people do not rebel against poisoning, genetic deformation, imminent total destruction.

Rather, people aspire to be top-managers no matter what the goods or services produced. One is a promoter, period; or a celebrity, period. The Gross National Product must increase without consideration of the standard of life. There is no natural limit, so the only security is in deterrence. The environment is rife with projected enemies. There is a huddling together

and conforming to avoid the vulnerability of any idio-
syncrasy, at the same time as each one has to be one-up
among his identical similars. Next, there is excitement
in identifying with the "really" powerful, the leaders,
the Great Nations, the decision-makers, dramatized on
the front page. But these leaders, of course, feel
equally powerless in the face of the Great Events. For
it is characteristic of the syndrome that as soon as there
is occasion for any practical activity, toward happiness, value, spirit, or even simple safety, everyone
suffers from the feeling of utter powerlessness; the internalized submissiveness now has its innings. Modern
technology is too complex; there is a population explosion; the computer will work out the proper war game
for us; they've got your number, don't stick your neck
out; "fallout is a physical fact of our nuclear age, it can
be faced like any other fact" (*Manual of Civil Defense*); "I'm strong, I can take sex or leave it" (eighteen-
year-old third-offender for felonious assault). In brief,
the underside of the psychology of power is that
Nothing Can Be Done; and the resolution of the stale-
mate is to explode. This is the Cold War.

I have frequently explored this psychology of proving, resignation, and catastrophic explosion (Wilhelm
Reich's "primary masochism"), and I shall not pursue
it again. It is filling the void of vital function by identifying with the agent that has frustrated it; with, subsequently, a strongly defended conceit, but panic when
any occasion calls for initiative, orginality, or even animal response. Here I have simply tried to relate this
psychology to the uncritical unanimous acceptance of
the idea of "getting into power in order to . . ." or
just "getting into power" as an end in itself. There is a
vicious circle, for (except in emergencies) the very
exercise of abstract power, managing and coercing, itself tends to stand in the way and alienate, to thwart

function and diminish energy, and so to increase the psychology of power. But of course the consequence of the process is to put us in fact in a continual emergency, so power creates its own need. I have tried to show how, historically, the psychology has been exacerbated by the miserable system of extrinsic motivation by incentives and punishments (including profits, wages, unemployment), reducing people to low-grade organisms no different from Professor Skinner's pigeons; whereas normal function is intrinsically motivated toward specific ends-in-view, and leads to growth in inventiveness and freedom. Where people are not directly in feelingful contact with what is to be done, nothing is done well and on time; they are always behind and the emergency becomes chronic. Even with good intentions, a few managers do not have enough *mind* for the needs of society—not even if their computers gallop through the calculations like lightning. I conclude that the consensus of recent political scientists that political theory is essentially the study of power-maneuvers, is itself a neurotic ideology. Normal politics has to do with the relations of specific functions in a community; and *such a study would often result in practical political inventions that would solve problems*—it would not merely predict elections and solve nothing, or play war games and destroy mankind.

Let me sum up these remarks in one homely and not newsy proposition: Throughout the world, it is bad domestic politics that creates the deadly international politics. Conversely, pacifism is revolutionary: we will not have peace unless there is a profound change in social structure, including getting rid of national sovereign power.

After this pedantic excursion, let me return, for a paragraph, to Professor Hughes. He does not have the psychology that Nothing Can Be Done, for he is doing something with immense energy. Indeed, his most valuable service, in my opinion, is to show that even in the framework of routine politics, there is a possible alternative mode of proceeding. (Adlai Stevenson, by contrast, never seemed to believe this.) Also, he obviously has no wish to "get into power" except precisely to stop the arms race and relax the Cold War. His campaign is primarily educational; and even if he were elected, I think, he would not feel that he has "power" but a splendid public forum. (This is the line of Kastenmeier and the Liberal Project Congressmen.)

Yet we cannot overlook the deep contradiction between peace and "getting into power" at all. With the strong background support of the unusually courageous New England professors, the hard work of politically renascent youth, and the total disgust of many of the electorate in the face of our insane policies, Professor Hughes has been able to by-pass the demoralizing and stupefying demands of the political clubhouse, or the emasculating horse's-ass-making requirements of rising to an important nomination through respectable channels. Nevertheless, the program with which he now appears before the electorate—I presume he means it sincerely—is inadequate to the needs of the situation. In foreign affairs, it is the kind of compromising that has no future. As a domestic program it is valueless, as if he had not put his mind to this as immediately important; yet it is just in this, in my view, that he could shake and begin to revive our people. And suppose he (or Szilard's candidates) were elected: he could hardly take a Constitutional oath to proceed to ring down the flag. Of course he has no such purpose, but nothing less will serve.

Concretely, our system of government at present comprises the military-industrial complex, the secret para-military agencies, the scientific war corporations, the blimps, the horses' asses, the police, the administrative bureaucracy, the career diplomats, the lobbies, the corporations that contribute Party funds, the underwriters and real-estate promoters that batten on Urban Renewal, the official press and the official opposition press, the sounding-off and jockeying for the next election, the National Unity, etc., etc. All this machine is grinding along by the momentum of the power and profit motives and style long since built into it; it *cannot* make decisions of a kind radically different than it does. Even if an excellent man happens to be elected to office, he will find that it is no longer a possible instrument for social change on any major issues of war and peace or the way of life of the Americans. Indeed, as the members of the Liberal Project have complained, office does not give even a good public forum, for the press does not report inconvenient speeches.

So we must look, finally, not to this kind of politics, but to direct functioning in what concerns us closely, in order to dispel the mesmerism of abstract power altogether. This has, of course, been the thinking of radical pacifism. The civil disobedience of the Committee for Nonviolent Action is the direct expression of each person's conscience of what it is impossible for him to live with. The studied withdrawal and boycotting advocated by the General Strike for Peace is a direct countering of the social drift toward catastrophe that occurs just because we cooperate with it. (The same holds for refusal in what is one's "private" important business, like the Women's Strike against poisoned milk or young men's refusing the draft.) Best of all, in principle, is the policy that Dave Dellinger espouses and tries to live by, to live communally and without authority, to work usefully and feel friendly, and so *positively to replace an area of power with peaceful functioning.* (Interestingly, even a critical and purgative group like *The Realist* is coming around to this point of view—with a hard row to hoe among urban poor people.) Similar is to work in foreign lands as a citizen of humanity, trying to avoid the Power blocs and their aims, *e.g.* the Friends Service. The merit of all these activities is that they produce a different kind of human relations and look to a different quality of life. This is a global and perhaps impossibly difficult task. But think. There is no history of mankind without these wars, which now have come to the maximum: can we have any hope except in a different kind of human relations?

It will be said that there is no time. Yes, probably. But let me cite a remark of Tocqueville. In his last work, *L'Ancien Régime*, he notes "with terror," as he says, how throughout the eighteenth century writer after writer and expert after expert pointed out that this and that detail of the Old Regime was unviable and could not possibly survive; added up, they proved that the entire Old Regime was doomed and must soon collapse; and yet *there was not a single man who foretold that there would be a mighty revolution.*

APPENDIX II

*Avoiding Responsibility**

1

There is a pattern of behavior in our corporate organization of society that, to me, is morally suffocating. Let me give two examples, one from the "private" sector and one from a public agency.

In the case of John Henry Faulk, the radio performer who was blacklisted, hounded, and deprived of livelihood, the broadcasting corporations were patently morally culpable. In Faulk's successful suit against the libelous conspiracy, it came out that important executives of CBS allowed themselves to be blackmailed, lied about the facts of the situation, did not confront Faulk or others with the charges against them, and indeed fired Faulk particularly as "controversial" because he was the one who openly fought for his civil rights.† CBS was substantially a member of the

---

* *Village Voice*, December 24, 1964.
† John Henry Faulk, *Fear on Trial* (New York: Simon and Schuster, November 1964).

conspiracy, but of course could not be brought to law for its merely moral derelictions. Faulk won a judgment of $3,000,000 against a small McCarthyite operator running a crummy private clearance business and against a fanatical chain-grocer; yet, to my knowledge, there has not been *any* apology to him or the public, or explanation, or offer of amends, on the part of CBS— or Young and Rubicam the advertisers, or the other broadcasters involved. Nevertheless, the stations of the CBS network appear before the FCC and apply for, and get, the renewal of their licenses to public channels *on the grounds that they are morally responsible organizations.* Because they are moral, they can be trusted as arbiters of mass communications; they can be trusted to give the public fair and reasonable coverage; and indeed, when there is any attempt to regulate their programming or policies, they howl censorship, for they are competent to regulate themselves.

Again, recently on the streets of New York a young Puerto Rican named Gregory Cruz was manhandled and shot down by a plainclothesman of ten years' experience. At once, the Police Department issued an official explanation that Cruz had resisted being questioned, had assaulted the officer, fled, etc. But the evidence is that Cruz took the cop for a mugger and was simply trying to get away.* Four unimpeachable eyewitnesses have stated that the police version is a total fabrication—there was no assault, etc.; and several others have come forth saying that the same cop stopped them without identifying himself. The cop has been suspended and the case is being investigated. And now the Deputy Police Commissioner, Walter Arm, says that Cruz was "an unfortunate victim of mistaken identity." It is not so. In this case, the policeman's be-

---

* The details of the Cruz case are given in the New York *World-Telegram,* October 9, 1964.

havior was habitual; and of course this case is similar to the many other cases, in all parts of the city, that have aroused outrage. It is evident that the police, either by indifference or policy, habitually behave in this way toward Negroes, Puerto Ricans, and other poor. Nevertheless, despite many proven instances of official lies, the police persist in their claim to be a morally responsible organization; they reject civilian review, they cover up pertinent information, etc.

In short, the pattern is as follows: *1.* The organization reduces its agents to personnel who carry out the organizational goals and policy. *2.* If something goes wrong and an agent is publicly exposed in an outrageous act, he suddenly becomes an individual person again and is so penalized. *3.* The organization takes no responsibility whatever, saves face, makes no public apology, makes no amends, does not look retroactively into similar past outrages that it has committed. *4.* Nevertheless, the organization blandly comes before the public as a morally responsible agent, with a right to regulate itself.

This pattern is ubiquitous in modern American society. It is, for me, finally unlivable.

2

Vested institutions, churches, and governments have always saved face, blandly lied, and maintained a solid front of moral legitimacy, the Establishment. Yet our present situation is different. On the one hand, the "real" morality, of persons, has an increasingly limited sphere of effectual public operation; corporate organization has now invaded every aspect of life to a degree that previously existed only in garrison states or explicit tyrannies; and indeed, the young have experienced nothing else. On the other hand, perhaps because of the difference in sheer quantity, there is a cynical or rationalizing acceptance of the corporate public-relations morality that is unique in history. Previously, in tyrannies, people either resigned themselves to the hypocritical double standard by regarding it as not human—as Southern Negroes came to regard the whites; or the pattern of hypocrisy was a grounds for radical dissent, reform movements, even revolution. And regimes remained legitimate by making a great show of purging themselves, shuffling officials, issuing White Papers. Nowadays, however, instead of alienation or rebellion, there is no questioning of the corporate behavior. People regard it as in the nature of things, and inevitably many people identify with it as right and proper. The organizations make the most perfunctory moral justification of themselves, or none at all, and *they are not expected to*. It is no doubt an odd thought to many readers that Mr. Stanton's dishonorable behavior during the blacklisting should make it problematic to continue to entrust him with public channels. Similarly, after the Quiz scandal, Mr. Van Doren was penalized, but Mr. Sarnoff of NBC resides in power and honor, although he was either an accomplice or entirely irresponsible.

Indeed, the evidence (collected by Robert Dubin) indicates that people take the corporations as their *model* of how to behave with beauty and dignity, but of course this model has no relation to their own *engaged* behavior, for in the corporations they are only personnel.

Under these circumstances there cannot be a legitimate Establishment and there cannot be citizens. Consider our state of affairs on the publication of the Warren Report. For a decade, lies of the CIA have been openly exposed, as in the U-2 incident; and forgeries in which the FBI has been involved have even been shown on national TV, as in the Army-McCarthy hearings. Yet in neither case has there been a moral compounding with the perpetrators nor any public outrage. What is the consequence? When the Warren Commission reports on the assassination of President Kennedy, any statements of the CIA and FBI—*e.g.* that Oswald was not an agent of theirs—are considered by critical people as of *no evidential value whatever,* and there is a presumption that "scientific" evidence produced by the Federal police may or may not be fabricated—one cannot tell! Yet there seems to be no public yearning for a renewal of trust. This *is* anomie. But it does not prevent J. Edgar Hoover from reading us sermons about delinquency and rioting in the streets.

I do not mean that popular indignation does not exist, nor that there is no justice to satisfy it. But the very form of the remedy underscores our dilemma and does nothing to alleviate it. Remedies and penalties are allotted to bare private individuals, stripped of their powers as functioning members of society or their corporate connections, but initiation and power continue to reside in the organizations and their personnel, that assume no responsibility. John Faulk is granted heavy damages and the crummy private investigator is penalized; but the case has not led to increasing the power of Faulk and his professional peers as a functioning group in broadcasting, nor has it changed public policy in the licensing of network stations. Similarly, Officer Devlin, the offending policeman, has been suspended for "excessive use of force," and hopefully young Mr. Cruz will collect damages for having spent four weeks on the critical list and losing the use of his right arm; but there is no indication whatever that there will be amends for all the *other* cases of police malfeasance that this one has cast light on, nor that the Commissioner of Police is eager to do justice in those other cases or change policy and practice for the future. (As I write this, there has been another incident, the murder of Eugene Forestier who, though handcuffed and beaten, apparently had to be shot by the two officers arresting him, to protect themselves.)

Such a method of remedy cannot clear the atmosphere. Indeed, instead of congratulating ourselves, as we do, on excellent decisions of the Supreme Court in civil liberties, we ought to be afraid. The Court is fighting a desperate rear-guard action to protect a few isolated individuals, while every other force of government and society is increasingly regimenting, brainwashing, coercing, and terrorizing as the regular course of events.

3

Frankly, I do not think there is a remedy within our present centralized style of social organization—the style of organizational goals, personnel, direction from headquarters, and chain of command. No matter how benevolent the goals, the style of execution is dehumanizing. So long as people are transformed into personnel—management-personnel, labor-personnel, professional-personnel—we cannot expect the organizations to be internally humanized by their persons, for there are no persons. (I need hardly draw the analogy to Eichmann.) And evidently there is little hope from external regulation, for the "citizenry" is likewise transformed, into consumer-personnel, client-personnel, and even voting-personnel. By and large, regulatory agencies come to an accommodation with the organizations they are supposed to regulate; and finally, the average person forgets what it is to make a human judgment and hope to be effective with it.

A hundred years ago, Karl Marx spoke of the mighty mystery by which useful objects were transformed into commodities whose value consisted only in buying and selling. We are now witnessing the even mightier mystery by which people are transformed into personnel, whose morality consists in organizational goals.

The live moral reaction is inevitably para-institutional, para-political, para-legal: sit-ins, boycotts, Beat withdrawal, demonstrations, riots, rising crime rate, drugs, etc. It is not easy to say how much of this is anomie, how much is what Arthur Waskow calls "creative disorder" or decentralized revolutionary activity, and how much is plain spite.

My own persisting opinion is that the only remedy for anomie is to give people more power to act effectively, and so to re-create *morale* and develop morals. This means, at present, to build into technology, urbanism, communications, politics, and education a strong admixture of decentral organization, in which people are not personnel but can initiate, decide, and cooperate. I have tried to show in a dozen works that this is not only generally feasible but would often be more efficient. Here let us just revert to the examples we started from.

There is no hope that the FCC can regulate Mr. Stanton or Mr. Sarnoff into becoming moral persons, for they are corporations; to frighten or harass them can only make them more devious, image-protecting, and tokenist. What the FCC can do, however, is to allocate the new channels so as to multiply independents and to encourage cooperative, artistic, professional, and folk control. AFTRA, the union of broadcasting people, correspondingly, can raise its vision beyond wages and featherbedding and take on the functions of a proper professional guild, to protect the professional integrity, good sense, and citizenly responsibility of its performers—all of which are sadly deranged by present broadcasting. And finally, the unaffiliated writers, artists, professors, experts, and other "personalities" on whom the networks heavily rely, can band together—perhaps under the coordination of the American Association of University Professors—to serve as a watchdog, boycotting when necessary.

To alleviate police brutality, the leaders of underprivileged groups have asked for civilian review boards on which they would be represented. This is certainly better than nothing, but it seems to me roundabout; and it is highly characteristic of the social style that causes our dilemmas: it does not try to dissolve the underlying alienation but adds on a new level of administration to regulate it. (Also, I am impressed by the claim of the police that it is impossible to carry on a dangerous function if unsympathetic supervisors are breathing down your neck. The result—as shown in Philadelphia—is bound to be a new accommodation between the police and the review boards; and the average person waits so long for his remedy, and must go through so much red tape, that it is as if he had no remedy.) It would be simpler and more direct to decentralize the policing of run-of-the-mill delinquencies to the neighborhoods themselves. Not only the policemen, but also the judgment of what is socially acceptable, should be drawn from the people who are policed. The aim of run-of-the-mill policing is to keep the peace, it is not to impose a "universal" standard, which indeed cannot be imposed but degenerates into payoffs.

APPENDIX III

Memorandum to
the Poverty Program

Three premises:
1. To cope with urban poverty is finally impossible in present excessive crowding. It takes a Park Avenue income to live decently in present Harlem density. (By 1980, 70 per cent will live in metropolitan urban areas.)
2. As social policy we ought to aim toward a higher rural-urban ratio—but not in terms of cash-crop farming. We ought not to let the farm way of life simply go down the drain. As it is, we are increasingly getting the symptoms of population explosion while vast areas are *de*populating. This makes no sense.
3. The conditions of underprivileged slum kids cannot adequately be coped with by upgrading the schools alone, especially if the overcrowding continues. What is needed, for shut-in horizons, is

something more akin to what the anthropologists call "culture shock."

Proposal:

To board three to six slum kids of ages ten to eleven with a marginal farmer in a depopulating area (*e.g.* northern Wisconsin, northern New York, Vermont, northern New Hampshire.)

The kids will go to a country school for an entire year, with an option to repeat. The program is voluntary.

The farmer has no responsibility except to feed them and not beat them. (In fact, they would take part in farm work in most cases.) Inspection by the County Agent.

If there are five or six kids, a job could be provided for an aged woman or man—from the city or rural locality—as housekeeper.

The immediate advantages are manifold:

1. To give farmers a source of cash by growing people.

2. To cut down overcrowding in city schools and avoid the need for building new schools for which there is no space. (A new school for twelve hundred in New York City costs $2,500,-000.)

3. To save the now under-used country schools in depopulating areas. And also upgrade them.

4. Radical improvement in the education of slum children. At present, a child of thirteen will not have been half a mile from home in his entire life. A radical change of environment is far more liberating than "upgrading" the curriculum.

5. 4-H has expressed interest in the chance of doing an exciting useful job in giving these children a social life and introducing them to a new world.

It enables 4-H to play a vital role in the problems of urban life.

6. Racial integration. (Preferably the kids would be mixed Negro, Spanish, white.)

I choose ages ten and eleven in order to avoid too early separation from even bad homes, and on the other hand, to avoid the problems of puberty. At this age, further, the receiving localities would have a chance to do something for integration without having to cope with difficult cases or emotional opposition in the community.

The program must be entirely voluntary. It should be possible to make it clear to Negro or Puerto Rican leaders that it is advantageous.

The hope, in the long run, is that a certain number of children will take to the new environment, perhaps opt for another year of it. And ultimately, that as many as 2 or 3 per cent will decide for the country as life career.

Rural reconstruction is possible on the basis of helping to solve urban problems.

Costs:

Such a program could really be covered by city school systems alone. *E.g.* this year in New York City it takes $700 (excluding capital costs) to keep one child in school. Such a sum, divided between farmer and local school, could give the farmer $1,600 for four kids (at $400), and the under-used school one teacher (at $6,000) for twenty kids (at $300).

Evidently the city schools will not give up the money, especially the State aid. Here the poverty program—or perhaps HEW—can provide the difference.

November 1964

Memorandum to
the Office of Education

Premises:

1. For many bright "under-achievers" it is not the curriculum and methods that are at fault, but their lack of interest in lessons and scholastic environment altogether. They need real products to show, not examinations that have been passed.

   Among the underprivileged this shows up as dropout of the obviously gifted. In the middle class, it tends to show up as emphasis on "social life" and performance far below ability.

2. The problem is what educational environment suits these bright youngsters, that is real field work. There are certain enterprises that can give a well-rounded intellectual apprenticeship: *e.g.* radio stations, newspapers, little theaters, photographic agencies, architecture and engineering offices.

   For these to be educational environments, the

professionals in charge must see to it that the youth works on the several aspects of the enterprise: technical, artistic, manual, social, humanistic.

3. Our society has a critical need for independent cultural media to countervail the present mass media of communications and bureaucratic offices of design. But, though necessary, such small independents seem to find it impossible to survive economically, and must in some way be subsidized. In general, the chief costs in these enterprises, that spell the difference between survival and failure, are for staff.

E.g. to run a Pacifica radio station with professional staff plus volunteers costs $38 an hour. Of the total cost of the Living Theater (New York City) about half was staff salary, twenty staff at Equity minimum of $40 a week.

4. There is continual demand for new construction of high schools to meet the overcrowding; and the Federal government is asked to share in the expense.

E.g. Chicago has just asked for twenty new high schools (at about $6,000,000 each) to accommodate forty thousand who do not have seats. Besides this capital cost, the operating expense in an urban high school is about $1,000 a year per student.

Proposal:

Instead of putting all the new capital and operating money into new schools, I propose supporting or underwriting existing or new non-scholastic educational environments for bright under-achieving youth. *E.g.* community radio stations, local newspapers, little theaters, design offices.

These would provide real social needs now not economically feasible, instead of passed (or failed) examinations by those who are not suited for the academic environment.

I am thinking of enterprises run by about six professionals and twenty to twenty-five apprentices of ages sixteen to twenty. The apprenticeship is to serve as an *alternative* to the last two years of high school (and perhaps first year of college).

Apprentices to be paid $20 a week, in lieu of the $1,000 a year for schooling. Enterprises to be further helped out of the capital costs saved from new school construction.

Remarks:

What is needed for such a program is an earnest search around the country for existing small independent enterprises that warrant supporting, *e.g.* country papers that could provide a more valuable service than they do (they are mainly Social Notes) if they had the staff.

Halleck Hoffman, the president of Pacifica radio federation, has expressed eagerness to provide or suggest professionals.

The program could be, in one way, regarded as a means of upgrading the present Job Training Corps program, providing educational opportunity for intellectually superior youth (and being a means of desegregation).

A preferable way of looking at the program is as aid to small businesses—giving the seed-money as part of an educational function.

Finally, after two or three years, many such apprentices will want to continue in college. I do not think it would be difficult to arrange for their admission.

Memorandum to the Ford Foundation

Premises:

1. Remedial efforts in education (*e.g.* remedial reading, curriculum improvement, adjusting to the style and language of the culture of poverty) uniformly neglect the sociological effect of the official school itself, the school building, the classroom routine.

2. For many children, and especially those not brought up in middle-class routines, the official school is frightening and makes the mind clamp and the tongue clam up. Some children learn to give token performances and pass examinations, but they assimilate little and do not grow.

3. Especially for the culturally deprived, education should be child-centered. The formal pre-set curriculum does more harm than good. What is most required is close contact with attentive adults who can show things and answer questions.

4. The current craze for "pre-school" preparation is again an effort at processing, and neglects the alternative of changing the school itself.

Proposal:

A demonstration of radically decentralized primary schools (ages six to twelve), to tiny units of thirty children and three adults.

These can be located in store fronts on the child's own street, or in settlement houses unused from 9 A.M. to 3 P.M. What is essential is easy passage in and out.

Given this high teacher-student ratio, there can be continuous use of the city itself as the educational background, its transit, its museums, homes, colleges, restaurants, business offices, etc. This exposure to the going life of middle-class society was the chief principle of Higher Horizons during its early successful period.

By radical decentralization, we can dispense almost entirely with administration costs and sharply diminish capital costs. Thus available money can be spent on teachers.

The need for many new teachers (or teaching assistants) can be met by recruiting in the graduating class of any university those who "like children, will pay attention to them, show them things, and answer their questions." Nothing more is required for primary education. Thousands of young college graduates are eager for such a job for a couple of years, and they are among the most vital; but these same young people are unlikely to take "education courses" or be willing to work in bureaucratic school structures.

Model:

The First Street School in the Lower East Side in

New York City is run on these principles—population one third Negro, one third Puerto Rican, one third "white." Teacher-pupil ratio is at present about one to seven, yet the total cost per pupil is about equivalent to that in the New York City public system. (This school is an offshoot of the Sollaberg Summerhill School in Stony Point, New York, the thought being that this free form of education is even more desirable for the poor.)

Remarks:

Such little street schools allow for close contact with the parents, who can be used as helpers (*e.g.* cook). Also with well-disposed knowledgeable adults in the neighborhood—*e.g.* the pharmacist—who can give special teaching and information. It is just this inter-penetration of city and school that is difficult in the official big schools, and that makes it hard for the young to grow up into the adult world.

Such little schools can be used to provide for the overflow in the present system, instead of continually building big new buildings.

For purposes of general assembly—bringing together several hundred children for a collective event—the small schools can use the auditoria of the present big schools.

To regularize and control the small schools, each school can have one official teacher on the usual license (at $6,000 for forty weeks), plus two assistants (at $4,000).

APPENDIX VI

*A New Deal for the Arts**

1

The recent closing of the Living Theater in New York for default on rent and taxes reminds us strongly of the plight of such enterprises in our society. It is hard to be decently poor and to venture in a style uniquely one's own. To Europeans this was our most famous advance-guard company, and at home it was at least the most notorious. Yet simple calculation shows that it was unviable both economically and artistically. The maximum number of seats an off-Broadway theater may have, if it is to be allowed to pay the "Equity minimum" subsistence-wage scale, is 299; because of the unavailability of real estate in New York City, the Living Theater seated about 170. Its weekly budget was $2,000, of which half went for the subsistence salaries. Thus, the theater would have had to sell out nearly every night at four dollars a ticket to meet the budget and get enough ahead to mount a new produc-

* *Commentary*, January 1964.

tion. (A new production costs eight to ten thousand dollars.)

The ticket price was out of line for an advance-guard theatre. The directors' original intention had been to keep half the seats at one dollar—for students, poor artists, beatniks. Worse, the pressure to have pretty immediate "successes" inevitably undermined the artistic intention, which was to provide new-theater experiences and present the best available new plays, in order to enliven the torpid mass audience and form a new audience. Since the indifference or disapproval of the incompetent New York reviewers was guaranteed, one had to rely on word of mouth; but this takes months, one could not wait. Hence the temptation was strong to be sensational, or to play voguish modern classics like Brecht—which prevented the formation of a loyal new audience. If by chance there was an eventual selling notice for a play, like the *New Yorker*'s rave for Jack Gelber's *The Connection* or *Life*'s spread for Kenneth H. Brown's *The Brig* (ironically, the theater went bankrupt when it had one of its modest hits), the audience would consist of tourists and mink coats or week-end Yalees. Worst of all, in order to cash in, it was necessary to keep repeating the successful play long beyond the interest of the directors or performers, and this undermined the original aim, which had been to do repertory. By and large, indeed, the most interesting evenings at the Living Theater were Mondays, when off-Broadway is dark and the stage was used for irregular performances or readings.

The Living Theater had a non-profit classification and sought foundation support. But somehow, though a couple of the great foundations have rather generously supported several dozen little theaters, no money was forthcoming for this liveliest one. It was rumored that the Living Theater's connection with the World-wide General Strike for Peace put the foundations off; Julian Beck and Judith Malina (Mrs. Beck), the directors, were in and out of jail on this issue and civil rights; also the theater itself was a resort of known pacifists, potheads, poets, and other punks. A representative of a great foundation complained to me that the Living Theater was not financially scrupulous; he was apparently surprised that it would pay its actors before its bills, or that artists would write bouncing checks to save the opening of a play that they had prepared for six weeks. Or maybe the lack of foundation support was just "mathematical," as Kafka said of the mischances of this world.

Needless to say, many have proposed the usual liberal solution for such problems: paste the problem on the wall and throw government money at it. Since the arts, like the poor, are worthy and neglected, there must be an Arts Council in Washington and a direct government subsidy. But I doubt that the Congress of the United States would be a more sophisticated or catholic patron than the foundations; we can hardly expect it—under the patriotic fire of Walter Winchell or Senator Eastland—to support potheads, Communists, pacifists, homosexuals, or "nigger-lovers." At best, officially sponsored theater would be sanitary, uplifting, or mass entertaining; it could not be corrosive, political, or intimately vulgar and popular. Artistically, official support of *new* theater would in all probability be positively damaging. Especially under an administration with a certain moneyed cultivation, like that of Governor Rockefeller in New York or that of the late President in Washington, the tendency is to support glamorous showcases like Lincoln Center or the proposed National Arts Center, that create in the public mind the illusion that this kind of thing, with its Big

Names, is the norm of living art. Every such enterprise makes it all the harder for the genuine, the modest, the outlandish, to live and breathe. (The case of the WPA theater of the thirties was different—and I shall return to it.)

In my opinion, there is an important role for direct government subsidy of theater, namely to underwrite standard classical repertory, of drama and opera, say up to 1940, a generation ago. This is simply part of the education of the young and is no different from supporting museums or schools. Such repertory provides good training for directors and performers, it gives interim employment, it can do little damage to new art, and, indeed, by raising the general level of the audience, it indirectly and powerfully helps new art.

2

How, then, can our society support necessary new ventures like the Living Theater? Let me make a proposal springing from an analysis of the structure of our contemporary institutions. The essence of our modern problem, as I see it, is that the growth of mass communications, the centralized decision-making in the big media, their heavy capitalization, their concentration by continual mergers, the inflated costs for overhead, public relations, and highly organized labor, and the vast common-denominator audiences sought and created for the efficient and profitable use of such investments—these things pre-empt the field and make it impossible for small, new, or dissenting enterprises to get a start and a fair hearing. Even more important, the big mass media interlock in their financing and echo one another in content and style; with one tale to tell, they swamp and outblare, and they effectually set definite limits to what can "normally" be thought, said, and felt.

It is hardly necessary to demonstrate all this, but I will just mention the usual headings. *1.* "News" is what is selected as newsworthy by a few men in a few news services; three almost identical broadcasting networks abstract from the same; and then it is abridged for the *Junior Scholastic.* Even for this news only sixty towns in America have competing newspapers (in 1900 there were six hundred). *2.* The publishing houses merge and their editorial choices are increasingly determined by tie-ins with book clubs, serialization in national magazines, Hollywood, paperback reprints. *3.* The Standard of Living, how to live decently, is what is shown in the ads in a few mass-circulation magazines and identically in the TV commercials; and movie sets of respectable life come from the same factories. *4.* The "important" in entertainment is what is slickly produced, elaborately promoted, and reviewed by the right dozen papers and national magazines. *5.* Political thought is the platforms of two major parties that agree on crucial issues like the Cold War and the expanding economy, and the Congress decides to abrogate equal time for the broadcasting of minority opinions. *6.* Public-service communications, *e.g.* educational TV, are tightly geared to the Establishment universities and the middle-of-the-road school boards.

Now some of this has real advantages, and anyway the whole complex represents one inevitable use of the technology and the national economy. Yet this whole complex is gravely problematical, so problematical, indeed, that it faces us with a constitutional crisis. For in such an atmosphere of uniform thought and feeling, and potential brainwashing, it is impossible to carry on a free, rather than a mass, democracy. The attempt to regulate the media by government agencies, like the FCC, does not work; and the outcry of censorship, though entirely hypocritical, is correct in principle.

(As the case is, however, the broadcasters themselves censor: they blacklist and they wipe out controversial tapes even though they have exclusive licenses to the channels.) It has been proposed that the government itself be used to counteract the debasing media—for instance by establishing a TV channel like the BBC or by publishing an official edition of classical American literature. This is wise if it refers to transmitting authoritative information and standard fare, but it is entirely irrelevant to the problem of helping the controversial and the new, for of course the government is part of the consensus that makes it hard for the controversial to gain an entry.

Therefore, to meet this constitutional and cultural crisis, let us look for a new principle in the structure of the danger itself, and let us suggest that *it is the responsibility of the mass media themselves to support, freed from their own direction, a countervailing force of independent and dissenting media of all kinds.* Since it is mainly the size of the common-denominator audience that constitutes the peril, conceive of a graduated tax on the audience size—of the broadcasting stations and networks, big newspapers and chains, national magazines, Hollywood, the publishing combinations— *to create a fund earmarked exclusively for the support of countervailing small media:* local newspapers, little theaters and magazines, unaffiliated broadcasters. The tax would be collected by local, State, or Federal government as relevant; we shall discuss the administration of the fund below. The constitutional virtue of this proposal is that it provides for the danger—of brainwashing—to generate its own antidote. Moreover, it is altogether in the spirit of the American principle of built-in checks and balances, applied to technical and economic conditions where free competition cannot work, where, indeed, there is semi-monopolistic private government paralleling or interlocked with public government.

As an immediate simple application of the principle to cases like the Living Theater, consider the following: Instead of repealing, as seems to be intended, the wartime excise tax on theater and movie tickets, earmark it for a fund to support little theater and experimental movies. This would in effect mean that the mass and commercial media, which provide almost all of the take, would be supporting the local, the offbeat, and the dissenting. I propose this immediate remedy because obviously it is easier and less painful to shift the use of an existing tax than to levy a new tax. But of course for the general application to the media—TV, press, advertising, and publishing—the rate (10 per cent per ticket) is vastly out of line. The aim of the proposed tax is *not* punitive or sumptuary or emergency, but simply to provide a steady modest revenue. We are concerned with audiences numbering often in the millions; an audience of a hundred thousand would surely be exempt. (Incidentally, there is now before the House of Commons a graduated tax on the advertising of the big broadcasting networks, but this seems to be partly punitive.)

3

To whom should support be given? I am strongly opposed to having arts councils or boards of experts as selectors. With the best will in the world, such experts are cliquish. Many of the best artists—as it turns out—are lacking in the character and techniques to win prestigious attention; they do not attend the right parties. Much that is excellent is overlooked or misunderstood; it sometimes wins its way unaided and is then crowned with help when it no longer needs any. The

thorny problem is to choose professionally—by definition, amateurs do not need "support"—and yet as ran-
domly as the spirit bloweth.

I have discussed the matter with Mr. and Mrs. Beck
of the Living Theater and we agree that the following
methods are tolerable: *1*. A popular principle: to divide
the country into regions and give aid to any group that
can get a certain number of thousand petitions for
itself. *2*. A professional principle: to support any
group that can win a certain number of dozen peers
as sponsors—namely directors, playwrights, professors
of literature or the humanities, critics, film-makers, etc.
These need not like what the group does, but must
be willing to testify that the enterprise is worthwhile
and should be helped to exist. *3*. Naturally, any group
that does exist in the present conditions has proved
its right to exist, and should be supported if necessary. *4*. Also, the old policy of the WPA theater
has much to recommend it: this was essentially to support everybody unemployed in the field; when there
were enough to form a group of any kind in a locality,
the group was underwritten and the individuals employed.

Support by the fund should be very modest, of no
interest to people in show business; and it should be
tailored just to help a worthwhile group get a hearing
and either try to win its way commercially or fulfill a
non-profit artistic function. Consider an interesting
case: Recently there was a little group at the Judson
Memorial Church (rent free) that passed a hat for the
scenery, lights, and ads; in my opinion, this group provided the best evenings of theater in New York City in
the past two years. It seems to me extremely important
for the dignity of such artists that they be paid Equity
minimum instead of nothing; and, of course, without
such pay no such group can persist. Or another kind of

case: the fund might underwrite a quarterly circulation of ten thousand copies for a little magazine for, say, three years, by which time it ought to have won its own audience or go out of business. Another case (to show how little money is involved): WBAI in New York City, certainly one of the best radio stations in the country, operates for $38 an hour (its salaries are low; most of its programming is volunteer). It has no ads. More than 60 per cent of its $250,000 budget comes from its twelve thousand subscribers, at $12 each. Yet the station might lapse because of the difficulty of getting gifts for the remainder. In this case, a subsidy of as little as $5 an hour would put everyone at ease.

Obviously, the fund must entail no responsibility either by or to the government. That is, it could subsidize activities politically extremist in any direction, morally questionable, or aesthetically outrageous, subject only to ordinary law.*

* The chief Congressional champion of aid to the arts is Rep. John Lindsay (R., N.Y.), and he too is earnestly insisting that a "Federal grant-in-aid program operated by a government-appointed panel should not dictate cultural tastes in America." I am quoting from his speech in the House of April 4, 1963. But affectionate as I am toward Congressman Lindsay, his proposal is a poor one, namely, that the government match funds with individual and foundation gifts above a certain minimum: "this would compel the organization to prove itself with the public before receiving government aid." If Mr. Lindsay thinks that rich individuals or foundations represent the public, or the artistic public, he does not know the facts of life. He moves too much in the right circles. "As a safeguard," he says, "a ceiling—say, 3 per cent of the total appropriation—should be set on the amount for any single organization. This would prevent a single group from capturing the whole Federal kitty." (But it would mean that thirty-five prestigious groups *would* capture it.) Lindsay entirely misses the point of how to support poverty-stricken authentic art. But at least he is trying. The problem is not perfectly soluble. For instance, there are probably some kinds of art which must *not* be helped, in order to remain themselves.

Allow me a philosophical reflection on the political principle that I am here using.

The justified suspicion of growing governmental power and the efforts to curtail it usually leave the field open to the operation of private powers that are almost as formidable and yet are less subject to popular check. The exercise and not very tender mercy of private powers are in turn met by the regulatory agencies and welfare policies of public power. Sometimes these public and private powers glower at each other and clinch, and then there is no social movement at all. At other times there are unholy combinations between them, like the military-industrial, government-universities, urban renewal–real estate promoter, politics–Madison Avenue complexes, that pre-empt the field, expand unchecked, ride roughshod, and exclude any independent, thrifty, or honest enterprise. Certainly, to avoid these dilemmas, we must encourage a different concept and practice of countervailing force. In important ways, public and private power do not usefully countervail each other when both are centralized and powerful, for the independent, the new, the dissenting are destroyed by both.

In a viable constitution, every excess of power should structurally generate its own antidote. That is, power entails a responsibility to counteract the dangers it creates—though proper exercise of the power should not thereby be impeded. In my opinion, resort to this kind of built-in countervalence is often far more direct and safer than relying on the intervention of the governmental juggernaut, whose bureaucracy, politicking, and policing are sometimes worse than the disease (if one is a "conservative") or are at best necessary evils (if one is a "liberal"). The proposal of a fund provided by the mass media to support independent media and prevent brainwashing is an example of built-in countervalence. (I think the same line of reasoning could be usefully pursued in another case: to make those who profit by automation more directly responsible to provide or educate for other employment or useful leisure.)

APPENDIX VII

*Engaged Editing**

1

We need information about the world that is practical, but what we get is the "news" of what has happened. The *Times*, AP, Reuters, or Tass guess what is important and the broadcasters and magazines follow their lead, but history goes its way regardless. Reporters are *then* hurriedly sent to the spot and the public learns the news. It turns to each blow after it has struck.

Reviewing *Liberation* as it turns into its tenth year, we see that this has not been its pattern. The topics it has treated are still with us and indeed are more in the "news" than when the articles were written and published. Let me give some examples. It did not generally seem in 1956, when the magazine started, that the para-political and sometimes para-legal demonstrations of

* This Preface to *Seeds of Liberation*, an anthology of writings that appeared originally in *Liberation* Magazine, is reprinted by permission of George Braziller, Inc. © 1964 by *Liberation*.

small groups could be of any historical importance. Especially nonviolence—sitting in front of trucks and filling jails—was strictly for the Hindoos. By 1956 there was a conspicuous rise of delinquency and anomie, but it was not yet fashionable to point out that the economy had a built-in structural defect; few noticed the hard-core poverty. And in the galloping growth of the Gross National Product and the drive to an affluent standard of living, it was simply "utopian" to raise questions about the moral and psychological worth of jobs and middle-class schooling, or about the human use of technology. It was not "realistic" to oppose bomb-testing and fallout shelters, nor to be alarmed that other powers beside NATO and the USSR would soon brandish atomic weapons. The news of the day did not yet take seriously the fact that the social revolution in the technologically underdeveloped regions of Latin America, Africa, and Asia would not so easily be contained in the policies of either the West or the USSR, but must become a new factor in the world. Finally, in 1956 we were at the beginning of the flood-tide of brilliant "social criticism" that has challenged every part of the American mores, from the I.Q.s and the advertising to the urbanism and the pesticides; yet for years almost all the criticism was negative; the few critics who doggedly proposed positive alternatives tended sooner or later to write for *Liberation.*

Thus, one could say that the "news" has been catching up to *Liberation.* And the implication might be that the editors of *Liberation* have some acute scientific theory that gives better predictions than the assumptions of the AP, Reuters, or Tass. But the editors have not told us this theory, and having sat at many of their meetings, I don't think there is any. If anything, they probably allow themselves to be more confused than the average, and they certainly have clashing opinions—though each one respects that the others must mean something or other.

In my opinion, the explanation of their editorial success is simpler. They are concerned. They deal with what they consider to be humanly important, and the factual test of importance is that they themselves get personally engaged in the events. In the long run—if one can stay alive—this must get one into closer touch with the underlying. Thus, Reuters might cover a bomb test in the Sahara as news (AP might not bother at all, it is so far away), but an editor of *Liberation* was with Africans trying to stop the test. And there is another aspect to such engaged editing: it is impossible to overlook injustice, ugliness, or stupidity that is gross and glaring, even though it is not "newsworthy" because it has persisted so long, people take it for granted, and it seems that nothing can or will be done about it. But if one is concerned, the more ingrained the offense the harder must one persist, for nothing is relevant except to get rid of it. This is very different from the *exposés* in the *New York Post* or one-shot conversation pieces in the *New Yorker*.

2

Perhaps *Liberation* does have a theory. It is the hopelessly indefinite one that human events are caused by and happen to human beings. As Kant pointed out, "What is Man?" is one of the unanswerable questions.

Such a theory has an oddly optimistic side. It means that vague aspiration, sudden indignation, animal perseverance, improbable fortitude, spontaneous invention, and even common sense are sometimes likely to become political factors, although both *realpolitik* and scientific sociology regard them as trivial. On this theory, it does not seem absurd to hope for social justice and love. Not that thoughts or sentiments have much effect, but that, beyond a certain point, reason flouted and feeling insulted do assert themselves, something in human nature is abiding; and since human beings are responsible for what they do and suffer, they might accept the responsibility.

But the theory also has a very dark side. For it means that it is impossible to blink away brutal human facts, no matter what fine explanations are given by statesmen, game theorists, and mathematical economists. For example, if a vast and increasing proportion of the wealth of nations is devoted to nuclear weapons, it is *not* possible to assume that we are not all going to be annihilated, and it is not possible to accept quietly the present world structure of Great Powers, even though it appears impossible to alter it. Somebody is responsible. If the hard core of poverty in fact rigidifies and increases in our present economic structure, it is not possible to be cheered by the Gross National Product, new technical marvels, or *communiqués* from the War on Poverty. And if the political and social style everywhere in the world is increasingly centralized, regimenting, and brainwashing, it is not possible to blink that we are heading toward 1984, even though this is nobody's "intention."

Because of its principle of engagement, *Liberation* is one of the few political groups—in the world—that takes for granted that social psychology exists and is about something, that social-psychological causes have political effects, just as, the Marxists hold, the political and economic structure has social-psychological effects. Let me again give an example. In the little *Tract for the Times* that introduced the first issue in 1956, there is a curious listing of the problems that Liberals have neglected: "War, poverty, boredom, authoritarianism, and other evils of modern times." Of

these, war and poverty are classical themes of radical
politics, but it is highly characteristic that boredom
and authoritarianism are mentioned with the same
status. Boredom, in 1956, partly referred to the era of
Eisenhower—it was a cliché of the Liberal columnists
—but to *Liberation* it also meant urban anomie, front
politics and public relations, mass communications, the
suburban standard of living. It was unusual at that time
to consider these things as political rather than aes-
thetic, but we are learning otherwise. Again, authoritarianism referred somewhat to dictatorships—though
Hitler, Mussolini, and Stalin were off the scene—but
even more, I think, the editors meant top-down direction in every sphere, whether parties, corporations, labor unions, families, or schools; they meant the reduction of democracy to democracy-by-consent, and the
"authoritarian personality" of the sociologists, with its
compulsions, prejudices, and need for petty triumphs.
These things are still not considered of political importance. We shall see.

To put it in a word, *Liberation* is edited authenti-
cally. Its news is not what is official, what is sensational
what will sell, what people are talking about, or what
suits a party program, but what the editors know is
relevant because they themselves cannot keep out of it,
and what they need to find out and report in order to
win allies.

Let me say at once, however, that this principle itself is problematic. You can certainly become so involved in events that you can't see straight. Consider,
by contrast, an amazing situation that we have gotten
used to: the police dog is attacking the child and the
TV cameraman is grinding away. This is dismaying,
yet in my judgment the professional journalist is not
necessarily in the wrong. The crucial question is an
existential one: Is he giving us the "news" or the

truth? And a related question, How in fact is the TV
viewer taking it, the moment before the scene changes
to the ad for tires that are like tiger's paws? (The
bother with "objective" journalism is that the audience
too is pretty "objective.")

This problem faces *Liberation* in a very concrete
form. The magazine has the defect of its virtue. The
editors are intelligent, energetic, craftsmanlike; they
are learned and have considerable literary ability. But
it is quite impossible to be at strategy meetings in India
and Sweden, to be sitting in assorted jails, to be visiting
Cuba by a circuitous route, to be on the executive
board of umpteen committees, to be organizing a mass
march, and to picket the Atomic Energy Commission,
and still do the desk work and correspondence necessary to turn out a consistently excellent magazine. It
does not help, either, that the magazine is (inevitably)
always in the red. I don't know any solution for this
dilemma.

3

Yet all this is mighty big talk for a very small and
not especially brilliant magazine, granting that it is in-
fluential beyond its circulation, and occasionally first
rate. A more accurate description of *Liberation* is that
it is the annals of people who, like the editors, put their
bodies on the line for justice as they see it and try to
live in community in a society that has given up on
community. *Liberation* is the house organ, so to speak,
where these people can get first-hand accounts of the
Times Square demonstration where the police rode
into the crowd, the sailing of a small boat into the nuclear test zone, a walk to Moscow to hand out leaflets,
the fortitude of the children of Birmingham, conditions in a Georgia jail, the founding of a small industry
among destitute sharecroppers, and education in a

Summerhill school. Recently, the magazine is being read—especially in colleges—by people who have become interested in these people and their activities.

Needless to say, these active people do not number in the millions or hundreds of thousands, nor does the readership of *Liberation*. Does this tiny fringe have much significance for the general future of the country and the world? I hope so—for usually these few people make sense; and alas! in crucial moments they sometimes make all the sense there is.

Looked at with a quick frank glance, *Liberation* is a very paradoxical magazine. On the one hand there are the remarkable surveys of world power (to my mind A. J. Muste is the keenest political analyst in America), the epochal manifesto of the Triple Revolution, the best reporting of Cuba that has appeared anywhere, the beautiful study of sexual morals by the English Friends, the thorough science of Gorden Christiansen on fallout; such things are the contents of a general national magazine of the first order. But on the other hand, there are sentimental accounts of the joy of solidarity, confessional breast-beating, small details of interpersonal conflict and reconciliation—the kind of thing that fills a parish newsletter. (One almost expects a social-notes column telling us where is Jim Peck this month, and where is Judith Malina, and has M. I. made up with B. L. since their quarrel on the Walk?) The idea of *Liberation* is, evidently, that there is no discrepancy between these tones, or at least that they are all of a piece.

As would be expected, the poetry in *Liberation* is the most accurate expression of how it is these days with intensely political and nonviolent humanists. The editors make no pretension to be "literary," they choose the verse entirely by feeling—what strikes them as interesting and meant. Thus, the poetry is a kind of projection of what they themselves mean when freed from the stoical or polemical necessities of political prose.

Unlike other "radical" poetry, the poems are almost entirely devoid of slogans, either affirmative or hostile. There is no party platform.

The content veers to two extremes that come to the same thing. Either there is a desperate affirmation of simple nature, including sexual love and childhood; or there is a total rejection of what man has done, in a tone sardonic or apocalyptic or violent. Sometimes there is a kind of deism, sometimes blasphemy.

But deeper than content is an acute self-awareness of a noteworthy kind, that seems to say, "I *accept* my responsibility, nevertheless I *can't.*" The tone of the self-awareness is noteworthy because it is not brooding, introspective, or self-pitying; yet, on the other hand, it is rarely self-condemning or sinful. Thus it is quite different from the usual self-consciousness in modern poetry, which is self-absorbed, self-ironical, self-judging, self-consoling, or embarrassed; but these people are *neither* in the right *nor* guilty.

To be in the right, to be moral, means to be adequate to the situation, to come across; good intentions are not enough; but the situation is too tough and therefore they are not in the right. Yet they are not guilty because they are not alienated, they do not make provisos or bargains, they do what they can. They are engaged—in an impasse. Creator spirit, come.

APPENDIX VIII

An Example of Spontaneous Administration*

1

It is interesting to see how the Columbia University Seminars have kept growing and have become a world-wide movement, yet entirely at variance with the way American institutions are supposed to succeed. Without money, publicity, or Organization, and following a course pretty uncompromisingly irrelevant to the needs of the front office, the seminar movement seems to have no other strength than that it is a good idea. Indeed, a candid look at the history shows that the idea itself was not what people meant at the beginning; it has developed according to its own logic. And today a knowing sociologist like Paul Lazarsfeld can speak of the "tragedy" of the Seminars' present course, whereas to others of us they are succeeding beyond expectation. It is a remarkable case.

The "Columbia University Seminars"—at present

* Expanded from "Columbia's Unorthodox Seminars," *Harper's*, January 1964.

they are not teaching seminars, though they were certainly meant to be so; the majority of the members are no longer from Columbia; and the most striking feature of the recent growth is the increase in the membership that is not even University! In 1945, when there were five seminars, almost all the members were from Columbia. By 1959 only half were from Columbia. Now, in 1964, of 801 members in 34 seminars, 418 are outsiders and 223 of these have no academic affiliation at all. There are 85 foreigners, including 33 from Europe, 33 from Asia, and 6 from Africa.

Beyond expectation, the Columbia Seminars have become a scholarly center for the entire Northeastern region. But also, through its outsiders, the idea has spread throughout the United States and overseas. As I leaf perfunctorily through this year's correspondence in Frank Tannenbaum's office, I find a letter from the UN about setting up seminars in Tokyo; another from the Weizmann Institute in Israel; another from the Academy of Arts and Sciences, the publishers of *Daedalus*, about seminars in connection with Boston University; another from the Organization of American States; another from the Australian National University at Canberra. (Some of these letters cast a sad light on the conditions of modern intellectual life. A professor wants to know how the finances are managed but says, "I realize that this information is probably confidential." Another wants to know "what degree of confidentiality is maintained at meetings, especially in dealing with public and contentious issues." Such is the Republic of Letters mid-twentieth century.)

Here is a big packet of minutes, published by Feltrinelli, from a Seminar on Labor at the University of Florence, founded by Mino Vianello who was in the Columbia Seminar on Labor. And here is a letter appointing the Columbia Seminar on the Renaissance to a kind of honorary citizenship of the University of Padua. Some of us have recently organized an Institute for Policy Studies in Washington, and the heart of it is a series of seminars of government people and scholars from outside of government, rather strictly modeled on the Columbia University Seminars.

All kinds of Big Names turn up in the correspondence as active associates or frequent participants: Zaffrula Khan, past president of the UN General Assembly; I. I. Rabi, the physicist; Paul Tillich, the theologian; Philip Jessup of the World Court; Kurt Goldstein, the psychiatrist, and Erich Fromm; Ashley Montagu, the anthropologist, and Margaret Mead; James Mitchell, when Secretary of Labor, and Arthur Goldberg, before he was Secretary of Labor and on the Supreme Court. Etc., etc. There are several dozens of stars, and often the brightest. Of course such a list does not prove that anybody is giving anything or getting anything out of it, yet one cannot but be struck by the richness of experience that is available at these colloquies if the Seminar idea is indeed working, that is, if the members get to know one another well enough over the years to be open with one another. They do keep attending, so they must find it worthwhile. In the Seminars I attend, the people are pretty frank and pretty cooperative. Certainly, when the different Seminars come to publish their minutes (if they ever get the money to collate and edit them!) we shall have an extraordinary library of dialogue. It will be of historical interest; it is not hard to show that some of these people have been deeply influenced by these conversations with one another.

In my opinion, what is most remarkable in this development has been its community anarchy, where both the communal need and the anarchy of control foster each other, almost like a proof of the theories of

Prince Kropotkin. The groups constitute themselves, choose their own members, make their own rules and agenda. From the beginning the Seminars have been under the guidance—one would hardly say "direction" —of Frank Tannenbaum, but his undeviating policy has been to keep the associations of scholars absolutely voluntary, self-ruled, and independent. There is no doubt that the force of the associations has been in their need and idea: the need for dialogue across disciplinary and academic boundaries, to explore our confusions: the unprecedented technology and urbanization and One World, the rigidifying isolated institutions that lose touch with the concrete wholeness of life, the excess of Knowledge that does not add up. When a new Seminar is planned, Frank Tannenbaum gives his advice as to what, in his experience, mechanically works out best with regard to numbers, meeting time, and so forth; he has a good nose for what constitutes an area of concern unified enough not to fall apart; he points out that the members ought to be people who might get to like one another; and if you need money for a member's train fare, he gives it if he has it or can scrounge it. Otherwise one hears little from Frank.

From the Columbia administration, to its credit, one hears nothing at all. The trustees send each outsider a lovely piece of paper appointing him a Seminar Associate, with library privileges and his name on the register for forwarding mail.

Probably essential for freedom is that the whole enterprise is run on a shoestring. The total expenses for 1962-63 came to $27,000 for about 450 meetings of 31 groups of distinguished people, some of whom got train fare. The chief item was $11,500 for secretaries, mostly graduate students, who operated the tape-recorders, etc. The printing of the minutes and notices

came to $4,000. The chief other expense was for the
meeting rooms, at $15 or $7.50, plus dinners for the
young secretaries and the guest speakers. This item has
caused Frank's secretary to complain that the Faculty
Club had a nerve to charge so much for the rooms
when the Seminars brought in so many people who paid
for dinner. In my opinion, it indicates the earnestness
of an enterprise that, when the meeting includes perhaps the President of the UN General Assembly, a
judge of the World Court, a nuclear physicist of crashing renown, etc., the concern backstage is about the
$15 for the room, or maybe $7.50! The great luxury of
the University Seminars was the Banquet, attended by
about 250—this came to $1,200.

For the total budget, Columbia contributes $10,000 a
year, plus a very plain office for Frank and his secretary. At the general meeting last year, the treasurer,
Albert G. Redpath, gave the following succinct finan-
cial report: "We are always in the red, but some of our
friends come to the rescue. We're in the red this year,
and I'm sure we'll be in the red next year."

In this style, the University Seminars have had a singularly pure and consistent history for a spiritual institution in modern America. As we shall see, they have
sloughed off what did not suit their inner logic and
they have grown without major compromise. They
have obviously been protected by complacent friends
in the Columbia administration, but in the main we
may say that here is one of those beautiful and rare
cases, like a fine little magazine or a little theater, run
on a shoestring, where voluntary effort simply pours
forth and produces great results because nobody inter-
feres and nobody has reservations about the motives of
the people or the worthwhileness of the purpose. Unfortunately, success itself has its dangers; people now
want to use you for your own good.

Here I want to discuss a kind of constitutional question: What *is* the Seminar movement as a new institution in the structure of American universities? What does it signify in modern intellectual life in general? And also, since there has increasingly become apparent in the movement a quiet but stubborn conflict of fundamental purpose between the poverty-stricken spontaneity and independence that Frank Tannenbaum has intuitively protected, and a more rational administrative approach aiming at power and effectiveness—what is the future of this?

2

Since the Seminars have no professors or students, Frank Tannenbaum keeps suggesting that the name be changed to *Collegia*, for "they are closer in spirit to those clusters of colleges about which the English universities have grown. . . . Ideally, each Seminar is a body of life-long 'fellows.' "

If I am not mistaken, the Professor of History's history is here faulty. Oxford University did not grow from its colleges, it was *superseded* by them. From the beginning in the thirteenth century, the University was the locus of the formal lectures by the regent masters; the colleges, when they became endowed, were mere residence halls. But with the growth of the New Learning—and perhaps, also, because the back of the University was broken by the King in suppressing the disturbances around Wycliffe—by the time of the Renaissance the medieval lectures had become quite irrelevant, and the young did not bother to leave their residences to hear them. It was the University that lapsed; the dissociated colleges of fellows survived. Is there anything analogous at present that the Seminars represent?

Certainly our American universities are not lapsing

—nor has the King broken their backs. On the contrary, their population is galloping, their buildings are growing grander, the funds from government, foundations, and corporations are rich indeed. Ph. D. theses fall like snow. There is a Knowledge Explosion. And far from staying home, the bright young people compete madly to climb the university ladder that leads to jobs, money, and prestige. (Perhaps the Division of Humanities *is* a bit irrelevant, and does not share in either the population nor the Knowledge Explosions —nor in the funds.)

Nevertheless, there is something wrong with out universities as communities of scholars, and many serious professionals and scientists—and, alas, many serious adolescents—are increasingly dissatisfied. A master of any art has a need and duty to teach, but teaching is discouraged by the rigmarole of courses and credits, not to speak of the absurdly swollen classes. Some masters feel that they can teach better by devoting themselves to their own research, with a few apprentices. The university stuffs the students with subjects and goads them with grading, but it fails to convey what the life of the intellect is about. (A professor of astronomy at Yale told me that he had excellent students, much cleverer mathematicians than he was; but not one of them, in his opinion, would be an astronomer. How was that? "They don't love the stars," he said.) Also, the masters no longer run the university; they have lost their autonomy to the grandiose administration and have become wage-slaves and time-servers. Since they are powerless, the faculty no longer communicate; and because they do not communicate, they are powerless. Rather, there has developed an academic personality, isolated, socially insecure, clinging to a narrow expertise to save face, and yet ridiculously arrogant and contemptuous of laymen. Certainly the specialist knowledge that pours out is terribly relevant in the world and avidly applied, both as scientific technology and social engineering, yet it does not seem to improve the world. As is the way of explosions, the Knowledge Explosion does not add up. Besides, a lot of what goes on at a university is busywork to prevent unemployment; a lot of it is a mechanical process of research running wild; and the problem-solving is often so mindless that it increases confusion and compounds the problems.

Prima facie, the University Seminars were designed as a specific academic remedy for many of these ills. They were dreamed up by professors and approved by a benevolent and worried wartime administration. The aim was to re-establish some kind of community and means of integrated teaching *within* the university. (This was, of course, before the astonishing postwar advent of contracted research and the total chaos of expansion.) The Seminar idea expressed the simple hunger of scholars to talk about what they care about, rather than suffering only the boredom of faculty parties—with spouses—or faculty meetings where nothing fundamental can be questioned, or mere shop talk with colleagues; and to engage in free exchange without having to maintain a jealous departmental courtesy and the caution, if not pretension, of the classroom. The students, in the original idea, would share in a more personal and less tutelary relation.

But we see that by now 60 per cent of the associates are not from Columbia at all (apparently, like one's family, one's university colleagues are not the company of choice); and "Oh, mercy," said a famous historian in one of the seminars, "let's not invite students to watch us flounder." Further, if the non-academics are now 25 per cent of the total and rapidly increasing, it is the academics who have invited them. To be sure,

the non-academics come because they believe, sometimes naïvely, that there is something liberal and humane at the university. On the whole, instead of a reform of the university, the Seminars seem to suggest a
spiritual withdrawal *from* the university, the formation of a different scholarly association.

Indeed, rather than Frank Tannenbaum's *collegia*,
the Seminars make one think of the scientific and
scholarly associations of the eighteenth century, before they became largely honorific or the hosts of annual conventions. The eighteenth-century associations
had no integral connection with the universities. We
do not think of Gibbon, Hume, Berkeley, Sam Johnson, William Jones, Lavoisier, Franklin, Voltaire,
Leibniz, Lessing, Rousseau, Goethe as academics. (The
great exception was Kant.) It has been an historical
accident of the last hundred fifty years that scholarship
became attached to the tutelage of adolescents, and
conversely, that the universities have become the centers of contemporary science. And interestingly, it is
just during the boom period of the American universities that the connection between research and teaching
begins to look untenable again. There is plenty of
money for research and development to be gotten
without teaching, both inside and outside the universities. (Except in the Humanities which, correspondingly, appear to be of little social significance.)

There is then need again for non-university associations of the learned, and I am suggesting that the Seminars might be such associations in embryo. But there is
a fascinating difference in intellectual morphology.
The new associations have to transcend departmental
disciplines. The eighteenth-century scientific academies flourished *before* the departmentalization of modern science. At that time the special disciplines existed
not as full-blown institutions with specifically trained

personnel and abstracted from the general enterprise of the life of reason; they shared the philosophic consensus of the Enlightenment (indeed, of the later Middle Ages), to which each man contributed as he could, often in several directions. At present, however, the departments constitute a rather rigid scholastic framework; each specialty has its trained priests and a most scrupulous ritual, its "own" method, in which research must be cast to be worthy of the name. This has advantages, but it is also true that once the specialties have developed there is usually no way of putting them together again. Experience which fits inconveniently into some slot in the framework is often neglected, or worse, it is ritually treated as if it did fit—the behavioral sciences consist largely of this. The desperate attempt to legislate *a priori* a Unified Language and method of Science results only in a more fatal lack of communication, because each discipline has its airtight postulate-sets. (In fact, the various scientists disregard the Unified Language.)

Consider a typical example. The policy of a modern city is worked up by its highway engineer, its houser, sociologist, school superintendent, tax expert, political administrator, architectural designer, etc., each in his expertness. When the whole is put together, it comes to delinquency, traffic congestion, crashing civic ugliness, etc.; but these too are then worked on as special problems, with new levels of administration, *ad hoc* programs for dropouts, face-lifting, one-way streets, and—needless to say—new millions of dollars for new kinds of experts. Nobody thinks of the community, the dialogue. (Or that too becomes a new kind of expert, the generalist!)

To counteract this kind of scholasticism, our mid-twentieth-century academies must be places where learned people can temporarily suspend their beautiful and useful methodic skills, that necessarily define too accurately and process and exclude too much beforehand, and where they can again confront, jointly, the raw, the concrete, the ongoing institution, the area, the era, the drift of change. This has from the beginning been the seminal inspiration of the Columbia Seminar movement, with its oddly assorted collections of the competent, and its list of awkward and rather vague themes: Peace, Rural Life, Problems of Interpretation, the Roles of the Health Professions, Technology and Social Change, Africa. One can envisage a lot of puzzled and worried people—Frank Tannenbaum speaks of "the splintered universe"—who are not at all sure what the boundaries of their problems are, but who are quite sure that these *are* the problems that must be faced by modern intellectuals.

This involves a characteristic attitude of mind. Let me pick out a couple of homely instances to illustrate it. In an account (1963) of the Seminar on Organization and Management, Professor Livingston said: "We had a very interesting report on a project here in Harlem where for forty blocks they have put together all the agencies that are taking care of welfare, public health, etc. The management problem when you put together a group of people loaned from different agencies, with different goals, different salaries, can become a serious issue in human relations. . . . Somebody pointed out that if you took the total budget that was spent, and divided it by the number of families taken care of, and then gave every one of these families $10,000 to get out of town, the city of New York would be saved a million dollars a year. I'm sure this isn't the answer, but at least this is a group that isn't bound by operationalism." Again, Dr. Molly Harrower, reporting for the Roles of the Health Professions (1962), explained that after six years the seminar had read through its minutes to get its bearings, and had suddenly discovered that it was necessary to think of the Patient who "in the words of one of our members, is the shock absorber of all administrative and professional failures." They therefore devoted the year to verbatim transcripts of hospital patients. (This led, however, to a speculation which, to my ear, has an ominous ring: "Can we draw up a blueprint for an additional yet undefined professional person . . . whose task will be to fill some of the startling gaps in patient care which we have jointly discovered?" This threatens a *new* level of professional failure!)

To my mind, these homely examples illustrate a grandiose point. The Division of Humanities is indeed moribund; academically it cannot survive in the Ph. D. system, and in society there are no longer paid places for humanists. The subjects studied in the division, Linguistics, Languages, Logic, Style, Classical Literature, History, etc., have become positive sciences like any others. But the Humanities must inevitably survive anyway, for they are, to paraphrase Matthew Arnold, the criticism of life. Maybe they can survive in these seminars.

3

The history at Columbia, as we look back over twenty years, has been surprising. A modern American university claims to have the two functions of Teaching and Research, and there is no doubt that the Seminars were supposed to help fulfill them directly, but they have not come across—and nevertheless the movement has grown.

First, the Seminars have withdrawn from "teaching." In the original formal proposal by the professors to Frank Fackenthal, then acting president (1944), of ten propositions, no fewer than five were concerned with the recruitment and examination of students, and the Seminars were empowered to give academic credit. Nevertheless by 1960 the astonishing language used in a report in the *Graduate Faculties Newsletter* is, "graduate students are excluded from the Seminars, and only in exceptional circumstances has a doctoral candidate been invited to sit in!" The statement is an exaggeration; graduate students are not "excluded," and there are always a few who follow their admired elders in and keep their mouths shut; but they are not sought, and, after a while, neither have they sought to come.

Of course this is a pity. What an opportunity for a Ph. D. candidate preparing a thesis, to present his idea to such a constellation of scholars and active professionals, for criticism, orientation, and bibliography! Yet this occurred only in the first years. The thing has developed according to its own logic.

Frank Tannenbaum's attitude on the students is characteristically ambiguous. On the one hand, ambitious for his project, he speaks of the Seminars as the basis of a new university, and he toys with the idea of paying graduate students to accompany their professors from Syracuse or M. I. T. He claims that the effectual exclusion is really a problem of space; there is no place for auditors in the rooms in the Faculty Club where most of the Seminars convene for dinner and discussion. On the other hand, he is quick to warn people that if they once begin to think in terms of credits and degrees, they are going to be tied up in administrative regulations, and that will be the end of liberty.

Again, the tangible (modern university) evidence for research is publication; and it was certainly the original expectation that these learned societies would promptly pour forth essays and books, the papers presented, the conclusions reached, collaborative research, sponsored research, vast volumes of minutes. Proposition 6 in the 1944 proposal reads, "The Seminar would in time, and the sooner the better, develop its own publication either from Seminar papers or from articles contributed by the staff, and we could project into the future a series of publications under the auspices of a Slavery Seminar at Columbia or the Seminar on Crime at Columbia, etc." (In fact there is no Seminar on Slavery or Crime.)

Especially at first there was some of all this. I could cite a respectable list of books, articles, whole issues of magazines, etc., that flowed from a Seminar, were dedicated to a Seminar, were attributed by the author to a Seminar. In fact, however, this kind of direct literary production has tended to decrease. As members come to know one another, their papers become less formal or they speak *ex tempore*. The essence is the dialogue. It is rediscovered that collaborative books are not usually a good idea, not so good as individual work assisted, as Professor Leary has put it, "by the recreation, reformation, testing and sharpening" of the community of peers. As Frank puts it, "Publication is not an immediate test. When men may ponder the same issue, complexities come to the surface and the search for understanding may be more important than a publication." Bravo! But I guess that the nadir of interest in publication was reached by the Seminar on Africa. When Frank complained that they had no minutes, they explained that they refused to take any "because it would be a bureaucratization of the extended family relation among ourselves!" This is more primitive than Socrates.

Another, less surprising development, has been the lack of resounding success in solving problems, though some of the Seminars were constituted just to solve particular problems. A typical explanation was given by I. I. Rabi: "Our Peace Seminar has the noble purpose of achieving peace. It has been operating for seventeen years, and sometimes I wish it would stop, because the conditions are getting worse and worse. After a while one doesn't talk about peace, one talks of tensions, and then not how to reduce them but how to describe them. We bring in more and more professional people and we become very good at describing a tense situation. Se we have not been very successful as a problem-solving institution."

4

By the same inner logic of development, some of the surprises have been happy. In an important sense, through these Seminars, Columbia is becoming the scholarly capital of the whole Eastern region and radiating through the world, as befits the major university of the greatest city in the West. For twenty years the Seminars have been an unexpected friendly resource for foreign scholars, either displaced or visiting, who might otherwise never have gotten to talk to anybody. They have been a means, rare in our universities, by which junior and senior faculty can get to know one another. And nowadays, when there is so much moving from school to school, the Seminars, just because they go beyond Columbia, have been a way of keeping in touch. And in the general speed-up, they have been a place where *emeriti* can continue academic connections and do their work. How poignantly these benefits reveal the conditions of modern life!

Here are some letters from non-academic associates. A request from an ancient dairy farmer: can he walk in the academic procession, as he has always wanted to do? A letter from Ashley Montagu: "As my only connection with any institution, I boast a great deal of my associateship with the Seminar on Genetics and the Evolution of Man." A letter I myself wrote a few years ago: "For a person who is no longer directly in academic life, it is a satisfying experience to take part in academic discussion of a high order. I cannot think of a better arrangement for maintaining the attitude *sub specie aeternitatis*." A letter from Thomas Coffin of NBC: "I especially approve the mingling of people from the academic and the commercial worlds."

A letter from Ruth Strang, when she was a professor of education at Teachers College: "It is certainly time, at my age, that I acquired patience and a less brusque manner. If the Seminar does that for me, it should get a good rating."

A remark of Professer Wallerstein: "Africa has become a fad, and during the UN session there are ten cocktail parties a week and five visiting presidents a month—and an incredible stream of State Department grants, Ford Foundation grants, University of London grants. It's a pleasure to come together under circumstances that make it possible to discuss anything seriously."

5

What then is the outlook for the future of this institution that operates on a shoestring and exists anomalously in a university great and cosmopolitan enough to cherish it, but where it does not really justify itself by tangible products of Teaching and Research? Yet on the other hand, it continues to grow on even a worldwide scale because it uniquely fills a need of modern culture.

"I have felt very lonely in this enterprise," grieved Frank, in a letter of 1956 to Lawrence Chamberlain, then Dean of the College. "The entire thing is so irregular that it is not easy to fit it into the forms for which University funds are traditionally available. Unless I can secure some kind of support, this whole development may one day be nipped in the bud."

The rational recipe for such a case is obvious: If you have a good product, sell it, making it shipshape and properly packaged to play an efficient role in American society, so that it can get proper support. This has been exactly the line taken recently by Paul Lazarsfeld, the sociologist, and Edward Bernays, who knows public relations. I cannot do better than to paraphrase their remarks. Professor Lazarsfeld loyally wants to sell the Seminars as part of Columbia, while Mr. Bernays wants to sell the Seminar movement to the world.

At the general meeting of the Seminars in 1962, Professor Lazarsfeld said that he was troubled that the Seminars were "not built into the academic and instructionary functions of the University." Not only was there a deplorable lack of graduate students, but at present there was an even more serious problem: there were more and more post-doctoral and foundation fellowships, that could not really be taught by the departments, but the Seminars were not being put to use for the purpose. And, even worse, he argued, there was a keen competition among the schools for these important post-Ph.Ds, and other schools often won out by offering more money. A way to attract these "important young scholars" was to make the resources of Columbia "visible." Only Columbia had Seminars, on the Renaissance, on Organization, on Mathematical Sociology; but they were invisible.

For example, President Kennedy had just spoken of the need to bring researchers and teachers in the behavioral sciences up to date on the new techniques, especially the use of computer methods; but the President had no way of knowing that there was exactly such a University Seminar at Columbia. "It is not visible," said Professor Lazarsfeld, "because it is not integrated into the University. There is not enough integration with graduate education, not enough organization, and not enough connection with the public relations program."

These were reasonable remarks, but they made one uneasy. As an outsider, I was not happy at the suggestion of being used to enhance Columbia's image; nor was the idea of academic competition for the scholars —and foundation money and military money—an easy one to admire. Also, government sponsorship did not seem the likeliest auspices for philosophic discourse.

Rising to answer Professor Lazarsfeld, Frank Tannenbaum repeated his litany: "This is a voluntary movement. Neither the president nor the dean nor the chairman of departments can run University Seminars; they run themselves. A Seminar ought to be able to take on graduate students if it is prepared and wants to. But if this were to become an administrative operation, the Seminar movement would ultimately wither away. What we've got here is a spontaneous grass-roots development which is terribly precious to the University, to American education, and to the individual members who participate in it."

Professor Lazarsfeld rejoined, "I don't feel this admiration for seventeen years of spontaneity. Frank Tannenbaum should now have a staff of people, and a Seminar that needs help shouldn't have to make him miserable because he doesn't have the money to pay a student's fare from Yale."

At the 1963 general meeting the issue inevitably arose again—inevitably, because our society is centralized and bureaucratized and rich, and the Seminars are decentralized and autonomous and poor; this time Frank's critical friend was Edward Bernays, a member of the Seminar on Public Communications.

Bernays developed the theme that America has always suffered from the deep cleavage and mutual hostility between its men of thought and its men of practical affairs. "But here at Columbia," he said, "there has been a growing body of proof that this dichotomy is obsolete." Therefore, the Seminars should be "expanded to meet the needs of the entire country" and to become "more visible." He offered five suggestions: organization of an American Committee for the Advancement of University Seminars; preparation of a memorandum to tell why University Seminars are vital; distribution of another manual of procedure based on the Columbia experience; sending a letter to the deans of faculty of the thousand colleges and universities listed in the *World Almanac;* briefing the great media of the country about the Seminars. Carried away, Bernays concluded by enthusiastically contributing a thousand dollars to the Frank Tannenbaum Fund, to put these plans into effect.

Frank confessed that he was flabbergasted, but managed to stammer, "It's a question how a movement of this kind can be made available. . . . Obviously our experience on this campus has shown its utility, or it wouldn't have survived nineteen years without outside support." Privately he said, "If a group of scholars don't know what they want, no dean can tell them."

6

The issue is a sober one. If a movement that has started out in its own style is to grow and be a force in society, must it end up in the same style as everything else, even though this takes the heart out of it?

If Professor Lazarsfeld's suggestions for organization were followed, there would soon likely be a majority of very different faces in the Seminars. Those who come for "recreation" would leave—the difference between recreation and work is not absence of earnestness or effort, but whether or not one does as one pleases and chooses the game. Men who are eager to share their knowledge would freeze and withdraw at a breath of competition for students. Some would be forced out because their contribution is "obstructive" or not constructive to the pre-ordained task that is not exactly their spontaneous choice. Professors who have not found a community in the regular American university would find they are still in the regular university. The outsiders who are invited would not be those profoundly esteemed as seminal spirits and companionable friends, or sometimes as strong contrasting colors, but those who have some skill for the task in hand, or prestige to attract "important young scholars" or the attention of Washington.

Nevertheless, it *is* a waste that there aren't more students, where there is so much erudition and experience for them to learn from. I am surprised, however, that the students themselves do not nag more vehemently to be invited. Can it be that the vast majority, including important young scholars, are not interested in learning their bearings, but just in getting ahead? I doubt that many of the associates would refuse them, up to a certain number, if they minded their manners.

Maybe the young could be included with no thought of credits or degrees. I realize that for many important young scholars this proposal is ridiculous.

Mr. Bernays' style of publicity is less virulent than Professor Lazarsfeld's efficient allocation of resources. It should do no harm to the associates unless they lose their sense of humor and begin to think of themselves as exemplars. And in provincial places, which follow

the lead of New York, to offer a description of the
Columbia Seminars might be useful, putting into form
what many professors and non-academic people
vaguely want but haven't thought through. Given Mr.
Bernays' usual success, however, it is easy to foresee
meetings of deans and chambers of commerce organizing spontaneous groups, while the trustees demand action in time for the new catalogue. Ultimately, the National Convention of University Seminars in Atlantic
City.

7

In any spontaneously administered community, it
seems to me, two factors are of major importance: the
power of the idea and need that makes the members
cooperate, and the nature—especially the social nature
—of the members. (A third important factor is a surrounding environment that allows the community to
live and breathe.) Let me end this little essay by saying
something about the social nature of Frank.

For twenty years now, Frank Tannenbaum has protected the Seminar movement from interference, while
it has developed according to its own logic and in response to a modern cultural need. The development
has been, we have seen, surprising. It was not expected
that the Seminars would be so entirely free of administrative control. It is to the honor of Columbia that it
has been a mansion for them.

It would be interesting to know by what arts Frank
blunts criticism, forestalls helpful interference, and
gets a modicum of support. I have not asked him. But I
was curious how he gravitated to this enterprise that
has become so much the life work of his later years.

He explained that when he was a student at Brook-
ings, there was a great deal of talking, and he was profoundly impressed by one incident. A visiting labor

leader sat down to breakfast at the cafeteria and a few students came to his table; at lunch he was still there in the center of a small crowd; by dinner he was still there in the center of a large crowd.

Later, in Washington, Frank used to have Tuesday evenings at home, with beer and pretzels in front of the fireplace. He would plan a set topic for discussion or have a star guest for people to pump. He was furious if people broke up into small conversations.

"Long before I went to college," says Frank, "I was enchanted with Plato's Socratic dialogues."

Frank is clearly a man with a vocation for University Seminars!

But he has another quality which, in my opinion, is even more relevant to a grass-roots and decentralist movement. Frank fancies himself as a dirt farmer, and he is full of stories about people who think that milk grows in bottles and who can't make do and take care of themselves. When we organized our Seminar on the City, we asked Frank to lead off as our first speaker. The subject that he obligingly chose was that all cities are a bad idea; real sense and independence, he said, spring up only in the country. This might not be the height of wisdom, but the man who can say it—in modern times—has stamina.

Institute for Policy Studies
Washington, D. C.

ABOUT THE AUTHOR

PAUL GOODMAN, a native New Yorker, was born in 1911. After graduating from City College in New York, he received his Ph.D. in humanities from the University of Chicago. Mr. Goodman has taught at the University of Chicago, New York University, Black Mountain College, Sarah Lawrence, and has lectured widely at various universities throughout the country. He is associated with the New York and Cleveland institutes for Gestalt Therapy and the University Seminar on Problems of Interpretation at Columbia. He is also a Fellow of the Institute for Policy Studies in Washington, D.C.

Mr. Goodman has written for *Commentary*, *Politics*, *Kenyon Review*, *Resistance*, *Liberation*, *Partisan Review*, etc. His fiction includes *The Facts of Life*, *The Break-Up of Our Camp*, *Parents' Day*, *The Empire City*, and *Making Do*, and he has also published a volume of verse, *The Lordly Hudson*. *Kafka's Prayer* and *The Structure of Literature* are books of criticism. In the area of social studies, in addition to being the co-author of *Communitas* and *Gestalt Therapy*, he has written *Art and Social Nature*, *Growing Up Absurd*, *Utopian Essays and Practical Proposals*, *Drawing the Line* (a pamphlet), *Community of Scholars*, and *Compulsory Mis-Education*.

Mr. Goodman is married and has three children.